Also by Theresa A. Morse

FUTURE A LA CARTE

Never in the Kitchen when Company Arrives

Never in the Kitchen

Doubleday & Company, Inc., Garden City,

THERESA A. MORSE

when Company Arrives

FOREWORD BY GAYNOR MADDOX

New York, 1 9 6 4

To my sisters **Helen** *and* **Jane**
and our adopted **Lizzie,**
with love

FOREWORD

Theresa Morse is an appetizing exception among writers of cookbooks. So many cook better than they can tell. Others write better than they know how to cook. But her gifted typewriter knows exactly what her mixing hand does.

She serves dinner with reticent gusto. I have relished countless of them. If I were her husband I would be jealous of her passion for the creative stove. When she cannot sleep I am sure she lulls herself to somnolence by counting the dishes she hopes to create tomorrow as they jump over the pantry fence. She awakes refreshed and the world eats better.

Tree Morse is an old friend. She is overpowering at times in her fierce determination to set everyone to eating better. She is a gastronomic moralist. To dine poorly, to fail to enjoy God's bounty, is downright sinful. That is her code and you will find it wonderful to swallow.

Her book catches her practical excitement over good food. Don't read it if you hope to escape the pleasures of planning, cooking, and serving unforgettable meals. Her recipes by their sheer excellence and her dedication to drudgery-free techniques will sweep you right through the kitchen. In these days of endless tension Theresa Morse believes that hospitality may be the last haven of human sanity and happiness.

GAYNOR MADDOX
(Food and Markets Editor of Newspaper
Enterprise Association, Inc.)

CONTENTS

Items followed by star (*) may be located by consulting the index.

INTRODUCTION

Who's Afraid of a Dinner Party?

At one time or another every hostess-cook is afraid of a dinner party, and no one who is honest will deny it. With six, eight, or a dozen people looking to you, and you alone, for delicious food and a delightful evening, life can be terrifying. No matter how helpful your man, the onus remains firmly attached to your shoulders. No one blames *him* if things go wrong.

How splendid if we could be born with a flair for cooking and entertaining, inherited from some talented ancestor, like Grandma. Failing that, however, there is comfort in the knowledge that these particular skills, unlike many, lie within the grasp of anyone wishing to acquire them.

The purpose of this book is twofold. First, to keep the hostess-cook, fearless and happy, out front where she belongs, from the minute the first guest arrives until ten minutes before serving, while dinner takes care of itself. Second, to make sure that dinner is delectable.

Obviously this cannot be accomplished by magic—all of us know only too well that desserts do not bake themselves, hors d'oeuvres do not assemble themselves, potatoes do not stuff themselves, ad infinitum.

However, there are tricks to any trade and cooking is no exception. Behind-the-scene strategy can spell the difference between nervous exhaustion and relaxed achievement. Exactly as an actress requires specific knowledge of stage techniques and direction, so does the hostess-cook require specific knowledge of menus, recipes, advance preparation and short cuts, if she hopes to produce wonderful food in a reasonable length of time. By this I mean the cook's time—not what goes on in an oven when a dish is on its own. That spectacular dessert, requiring an entire morning of slaving, is not for me. I'll settle for the beauty that melts in the mouth but requires only fifteen or twenty minutes to prepare. Astonishing what wonders can be produced in that length of time.

Mine is a split-cooking personality. From late May until early October my husband and I operate a small, informal inn (twelve guests at a time) on Martha's Vineyard. Doctors, lawyers, businessmen, professors, young executives, seasoned judges, writers, editors—all these and more besides, together with their wives, arrive at our door, bringing with them their preferences and dislikes, their charms and idiosyncrasies. They come to us entirely by word-of-mouth advertising, but we are well aware that no matter how comfortable the beds, congenial the company, or accessible the beaches—if the food is not consistently delicious, all else pales into insignificance. Listen in on any conversation at any holiday resort. Chances are that you will find food and weather competing for first place, with food way out in front.

Our inn is run along the lines of a home filled with guests, as far as the food is concerned. Thus we offer no choice of dishes except at breakfast where, each morning, we run the gamut of garden-herb omelets to fresh-caught broiled fish to pancakes, sausages, and maple syrup, with every conceivable item between. For the other meals, we inquire of newcomers as to their hates or allergies and are guided accordingly.

For the balance of the year I am a hostess-cook, keeping house for my husband (our children now have homes of their own), entertaining family and friends, and coping with the universal problem of how to produce tempting, delectable food and, at the same time, double as a relaxed hostess with nothing more pressing on her mind than welcoming guests and enjoying their company.

Through catering to our varied and assorted guests, we have learned the foods and combinations of food that delight prac-

tically everyone. The menus and recipes that will appear
shortly, are based largely on these findings.

This book will include the best of what I have learned from
housekeeping, innkeeping, and a winter spent at The Cordon
Bleu School of Cookery in London. Anything and everything
that will heighten interest and ease the way into the fascinating
world of food and hospitality. Lovely to look at, delicious to
eat, easy to make, *and* adaptable to beforehand preparation is
my yardstick for party fare.

PART ONE

Easy Entertaining

1

Kitchen Tranquilizers

Since it is almost as difficult to talk fluently in a foreign language, without benefit of grammar, as to cook a superb dinner, without benefit of basic aids to efficiency and peace of mind, I am listing those of the latter that mean the most to me.

A Modern Attractive Kitchen

It stands to reason that if your kitchen is a well-planned workshop rather than a booby trap filled with pitfalls, your lot will be an easier one. Make the most of what you have (no matter how small) and don't hesitate to call in kitchen consultants. These experts have brilliant ideas on the use of space and can save hundreds of kitchen steps per day, not to mention precious energy. They will also lend an attentive ear to a client's special preferences and act accordingly. I, for example, happen to be a pegboard fiend, and consider a kitchen with less than two knife magnets, lacking in bare essentials.

Indispensable Kitchen Equipment

A reliable stove, dependable oven thermometer, sharp knives, time clock, and all other basic kitchen equipment are as vital to a hostess-cook as an oxygen mask to a diver. Even if you are an old hand at cooking, you might find it helpful to check your equipment against the suggested tools in new (paperback) editions of any standard cookbook. From time to time new inventions, designed to speed or facilitate kitchen operations, creep into these lists, so it is seldom a total loss.

X Marks the Spot

"A place for everything and everything in its place" is a life-saving bromide when applied to kitchens. When the hand darts out for pepper mill, spices, herbs, monosodium glutamate . . . what comfort to find them on the precise spot where they belong and where you expect them to be. What frustration when they have vanished.

The Open-Shelves Policy

Open shelves, in tiers along the wall, close to the work space, are better than tranquilizers. Mine hold pint- and quart-sized jars with screw-on tops, labeled with bright-red nail polish, and containing those items used most often and a nuisance to dig out from behind closed cupboards. Such as: sugar of all kinds, bread crumbs, ground almonds, rice, marinades, oils, and vinegars. Thus, when a recipe calls for "½ cup dark-brown sugar," not only is it at hand, but quickly and easily extricated.

Case for the Clean Damp Cloth

Try this just once and chances are you will be an addict for life. On entering your kitchen with intent to toil, before tackling a single operation, take a clean, heavy dishcloth, rinse under cold water, wring out tightly, and deposit on a small, clean pan on your work space, at your elbow. The cloth is now available for wiping sticky hands (yours), used knives or other tools, for keeping work space clean, or shoving egg shells, sandwich crusts, and the like into that handy pan. No running back and forth to sink or garbage pail, no messy work space, and your knives are back on the magnet in a flash instead of languishing in the sink (a most unhealthy place for them).

Care and Distribution of Recipes

A recipe box is to a cook what a Stillson wrench is to a plumber, unless she happens to have the gift of total recall. Although this point has been belabored in magazines and cookbooks throughout the land, it is remarkable how many fine recipes can still be found crumpled in the back of kitchen drawers or stuck in dilapidated old cookbooks. This in spite of the fact that inability to find a wanted recipe can induce frenzy, bordering on temporary insanity. Anybody's family can furnish proof.

Now that I have gone on record in support of recipe boxes, I'd like to mention a few specific recommendations that make them easier to use:

Include in your box *only* those recipes that you have successfully made. Have a separate box for the ones that "look wonderful" but that you haven't had a chance to try. *Make them earn their way in.*

Note on the recipe card any additional information or changes stemming from your own experience. Such as "leave in oven extra 15 minutes," "baste with sherry," or "enough for 6 but double sauce."

Copy from your cookbooks those recipes that are great favorites and used often. It is much simpler to have one central source. Don't include those that are marvelous but seldom used (such as rich desserts). Instead, make a note on the front flyleaf of the name and page number.

One last suggestion—*Don't be stingy with your recipes.* Give them to anyone who asks for them. There is no finer compliment that a guest can pay than to ask longingly for the recipe of something she is eating at your table. As for the one who grudgingly says, "I'll give you this recipe if you promise not to tell a soul—" Beware! Danger on all fronts.

Board Rules and Regulations

There is no law requiring a large, stationary, wooden chopping board as part of everyone's kitchen work space, but I'd gladly vote for it. That is, if you have room for it. No matter how big a portable one, it is never big enough, is guaranteed to slip and slide, must be taken out when needed, and later put back where it belongs. Compare this to a large, stationary one, always at hand for trimming sandwiches, chopping vegetables, slicing bread, and dozens of other operations. Even if you live in formican splendor, a wooden board is essential for the well-being of your knife blades. So, for that matter, is the *open*, magnetic kniferack since knives dull in kitchen drawers and are easily nicked. (As far as I'm concerned, fitted, slotted knife holders were designed expressly for the purpose of inducing trauma.)

The Big Three

For outsized nuisances on the day before (or day of) a party, chopped nuts, chopped onions, and fresh, chopped parsley can't be beat. That is, if you happen to need them and party recipes usually call for one or all of them, especially the parsley.* As for the other two—frozen, chopped onions are now available in commercial packages at most supermarkets and can be used, either for cooking or adding to a dish, without a moment's defrosting. Nuts (walnuts or pecans) can be bought by the pound in broken pieces, chopped a bit more if desired, and stored in a tightly closed jar in the refrigerator. (If you have freezer space—buy several pounds and freeze them, too.) With these three ready and waiting, you can tackle almost anything.

Minor Maneuvers

Dinner parties are guaranteed to keep hostess-cooks hopping, but there are impedimenta to cooking that need not clog her path, once she is in action.

FLOUR: Keep two flour canisters, side by side, on the counter —one marked: SIFTED. Into this one sift one half of your bag of all-purpose flour when it arrives from the grocery store. Into the other, deposit the rest. Some recipes call for one, some the other, but having sifted flour on tap can save a good many separate jobs of sifting and clean-up for each five or ten pounds of flour.

When sifting flour with other ingredients (like baking powder or spices) for a specific recipe, do so on wax paper which can be thrown away.

SUGAR: Sift granulated sugar on to waxed paper, also. Keep powdered sugar in shaker, containing a split vanilla bean, to have on hand for dusting cookies or fresh-baked cake. Both fragrant and delicious. Soften caked, brown sugar by putting a piece of fresh bread into the container.

BREAD: To cut bread very thin—chill first in the refrigerator. To butter bread—have butter at room temperature.
To butter very thin bread—cut off the end of the loaf and butter each new surface before slicing.

ROAST MEAT: To avoid either uncertainty or catastrophe—use a *meat thermometer*.

CLEAN AS YOU GO: This is the last, but probably the most important of all suggestions in this chapter. For charm and satisfaction, it ranks second only to pay as you go. Kitchen utensils have an eerie way of multiplying in the sink exactly like unpaid bills in the desk.

2

Time to Entertain

The hour has struck. What seemed a simple, social act when you issued dinner invitations just a few short weeks ago now looms up as a nightmare. No matter how it came to pass, the indisputable fact remains that several people are looking to you, and you alone, for a delicious dinner just two days hence.

There's the saving grace. Take it easy, there is plenty of time to plan ahead. While this is considered fine strategy for tackling almost anything, when it comes to preparing a dinner party, there is no alternative. That is, not if you want to attend the party with something more than your battered, physical presence.

Conducive to hostess-cook comfort and peace of mind are:

A Hostess Book

This is a great tool. In an ordinary notebook (although elegant hostess books can be purchased and make unusual and welcome gifts) record the date of every dinner party, big or little; the guest list (noting both acceptances and refusals—this can be useful information at a later date); the menu (thus sparing yourself the agony of trying to remember former ones and risking repetition); the wines; and the flowers or decorations (if they happen to be extraordinary).

A Hostess Helper

If the success or failure of your dinner party depends exclusively on you (plus the loyal, helpful backing of your man, who may be a gem or whose nervous fluttering can drive you mad)—hire someone to assist you on the evening of the party if you possibly can. Maybe she won't know the first thing about cooking, maybe she's just a high school girl, but if she's willing, clean, and helpful, you are in luck. Interest her in what you are trying to accomplish, train her to perform those time-consuming jobs like basting chickens, heating rolls, warming plates, filling water glasses, and dozens of others, not forgetting the most important of all—assisting you during the dinner, and cleaning up afterwards. Hard work lies ahead, but the bare knowledge that, come five or six on THE day, someone will walk in the door whose sole job is to make life easier for you, will sustain you through almost anything.

Hostess-Cook Rules and Regulations

Prepare written menu and marketing list simultaneously and well in advance. Include everything from linen to cigarettes.

Make certain that your menu is not too ambitious nor too filling. Keep in mind contrasts in texture as well as nice balance between sweet and sour, crisp and soft, dark and light, in the food you are serving.

No dishes that you have not previously prepared.

No dishes that will spoil if guests are late.

No last-minute sauces.

No oven dishes requiring different temperatures at the same time.

Prepare a written work sheet for the day before and the day of the party. Apart from the obvious advantages, the pleasure of crossing off item after item compares favorably to this same procedure during Christmas shopping.

Warm plates for hot food.

For the hostess-cook with a helper, a large buffet party with guests seated at small tables is easy to handle. Provided that the tables are set as though for a sit-down dinner, complete with silver, linen, water, cigarettes, ash trays, etc., and the guests are obliged to carry nothing more burdensome than a warm plate piled high with delicious food of their own choosing.

Right here is a danger zone. Drinks over, the hostess hospitably urges her guests to the buffet table and, while the men politely hold back, the women form a line and begin selecting food. At this moment the party begins to disintegrate. Surely you have stood in such a line. Once your food is assembled, you cast about for a place to sit. Often small tables are spread out over two or three rooms with no sign of place cards (which, in the general confusion, you couldn't find anyhow). So you settle into a vacant seat, hoping that a congenial male will find his way to your side. What invariably turns up is the one man you would like to avoid. By this time your food is cold and so are your spirits.

How much nicer if the hostess, when announcing dinner, assigns partners and invites her guests to travel down the buffet in pairs. How much gayer a party if the very man you would have chosen (smart hostesses develop a talent for compatible seating arrangements) claims you as his partner, escorts you down the buffet and guides you to a table where, together, you begin eating that hot, delicious food. It will no longer matter who sits on the other side.

In the event that you do not have a helper, large buffets and scattered tables are difficult to handle. All goes well during the main course, but dessert and coffee present problems. With no helper to clear the tables, inevitably the men rise, collect the dirty dishes, deposit them on the once-lovely buffet, pick up dessert and coffee, bumble back to the table, and think longingly of the comforts of home.

Hence, without a helper, it is far easier for a hostess-cook to manage small dinners of six or eight. Serve the food on a buffet table, as before, but have all the guests seated at one table, complete with place cards (or announce a seating arrangement).

Now, when the main course is finished, the hostess is in a position to control the next step. *Don't let your guests rise from the table to assist with the clearing off.* Nothing dampens the spirit of a good party more effectively than the mass exodus of the ladies present, clutching dirty dishes and heading for the kitchen. A friend of mine worked out an excellent solution.

"Clark takes everything *out*, and I bring everything *in*," she told me. While he is clearing off the table (with the help of a cart on wheels), she remains seated with her guests. When he returns to the table, she slips out to the kitchen and wheels in dessert and coffee. (In our household the code word "Clark" is enough to get my husband on his feet.)

Don't, under any circumstances, permit your guests to help after dinner, either. I do not refer to those evenings when you are entertaining your two closest friends and, while the men talk shop, the ladies, leisurely and chattily, do the dishes. I am talking about a party where guests, in festive mood, wearing attractive clothes, have come to your house for dinner. "It will take only a minute," they will say, and "many hands—" Besides, they "love to help."

Don't listen. They do not mean one word they are saying, so just whisk them out of the dining area as fast as you can, and close the door on the debris. After the last guest has departed, you and your husband tackle the mess any way you choose.

The menus that follow are designed to get you out of the kitchen and into the living room in time to greet the first arrivals and enjoy a cocktail or two with nothing on your mind. Later, when the party is under way (drinks should be leisurely but not endless), you will have to return to the kitchen for a few minutes in order to taste, garnish, toss— whatever remains to be done that, helper or no, you prefer doing yourself.

Dinner is ready. Like Election Day morning, there is nothing further the candidate can do to win victory. *Que sera sera.* The sound of laughter is reassuring, and sparkling repartee gives further proof that the party is going well. But nothing, absolutely nothing, will provide the exhilaration that comes from those seven magical words, "This is the best I've ever tasted," spoken by dinner guests at your table.

3

Please Help Yourself to Appetizers

The cocktail interval before dinner not only provides immediate, warming hospitality, but enables the hostess-cook to serve the equivalent of a first course, which otherwise would be difficult to manage.

For some guests, this is the best part of the dinner. Others consider anything heartier than nibbles of vegetables, olives, or tiny crackers, a menace designed to spoil appetites for the dinner that follows. Still others behave as though the calories involved in these particular viands are damaging to avoirdupois above all others.

If you know the tastes and preferences of your guests in this area, be guided accordingly. If entertaining calorie counters, don't mow them down with temptation. If starving young men, go overboard. If you are uncertain (usually the case) try to have enough variety to appeal to everyone. In any case, have the appetizers conveniently at hand, urge your guests to help themselves, then leave them alone.

When the cocktail hour first gets under way, I am always among those present. Long ago I discovered that if I'm out in the kitchen, broiling delicious tidbits, while my guests are cozily bending their elbows, I get a Cinderella-type feeling. So, unless a helper is in the kitchen to mind the appetizers, I limit myself to those that are tasty without benefit of oven. Or hot plates, on which, all too quickly, they seem to acquire a bedraggled look.

In the recipes that follow, quantities are given for dinners of six. But you know your guests, so add or subtract as you see fit.

SALTED ALMONDS

> ½ pound blanched whole almonds
>> If unable to purchase them blanched, drop into boiling water and let stand 3–4 minutes. The skins will then slip off quickly and easily
> 2 tablespoons olive oil or melted butter
> Sugar and salt

350-DEGREE OVEN

Place almonds on a closed cookie tin, pour over the oil (or butter), and turn with a tablespoon until nuts are well coated. Place in the 350-degree oven for about 30 minutes, turning occasionally so that they can brown evenly. When a medium brown on all sides, remove from oven and spread out on paper toweling. Immediately sprinkle generously with salt and sparingly with sugar (about ½ teaspoon), turning the nuts a few times. Let stand about 5 minutes, then pour into a brown-paper bag (which will absorb any remaining oil) and let cool. Leave them in the bag until ready to serve.

MARINATED PITTED RIPE OLIVES

> 1 four-ounce jar pitted ripe olives
> ½ tablespoon olive oil
> 1 clove of garlic

Drain the olives and put in a bowl. Spoon over the olive oil and turn lightly to coat. Add clove of garlic and marinate overnight. When ready to serve, remove garlic clove and drain. These make a nice decoration for the Nova Scotia salmon appetizer to follow, or are very good by themselves.

STUFFED NOVA SCOTIA SALMON

*1 three-ounce package
cream cheese*
1 teaspoon sour cream
*8 slices Nova Scotia
salmon*

*1 tablespoon fresh lemon
juice*
Fresh-ground pepper

Blend together the cream cheese and sour cream until of spreading consistency. Trim the uneven edges of the salmon, sprinkle each slice with lemon juice and pepper, then spread with cheese. Roll up tight and slice into bite-sized pieces.

CURRIED STUFFED EGGS

*6 small, hard-cooked eggs,
shelled*
2 tablespoons mayonnaise
Fresh lemon juice

Curry powder
Salt and pepper
Chopped parsley
Sliced stuffed olives

Cut the eggs in two (the long way), remove the yolks and place in a bowl, put egg whites on a platter. Mash the yolks well with a fork. Season the mayonnaise with lemon juice and curry powder (to taste), and add to yolks. Season mixture with salt and pepper, add a sprinkling of parsley, and spoon into whites. Make a crisscross pattern across the top with the back of the fork and garnish each half with slices of olive (or caviar, if you happen to have some on hand).

BALLS TARTARE

*½ pound top round or
sirloin, ground twice*
¼ pound fresh sauerkraut

Salt and pepper
½ teaspoon caraway seeds
Chopped chives or parsley

Season the meat and form into 24 flat rounds. Drain the sauerkraut, chop very fine, and add the caraway seeds. Place ½ teaspoon of this mixture on each meat round and fold the meat over so that it entirely encloses the sauerkraut. Shape into small balls and roll in finely chopped chives or parsley. Chill in refrigerator until ready to serve. Have small glass filled with toothpicks on the platter.

GEORGE'S MUSHROOM CAVIAR

(Can be made the day before)

½ medium-sized onion,
    minced
1 tablespoon butter
¼ pound fresh
    mushrooms, chopped
    fine
1 tablespoon lemon juice

½ teaspoon
    Worcestershire sauce
Mayonnaise (enough to
    hold mixture
    together)
Salt and fresh-ground
    pepper

Sauté onion in the butter until golden. Add mushrooms and sauté for 5 minutes, stirring lightly to mix well. Add lemon juice and Worcestershire sauce, mix well and remove from stove. Add enough mayonnaise to bind and then mound on a serving plate. Chill well and serve surrounded by Melba toast or any bland crackers.

STUFFED MUSHROOMS

18 medium-sized,
    perfectly shaped
    mushrooms
1 three-ounce package of
    cream cheese

1 tablespoon sour cream
Anchovy paste
Fresh, chopped chives
Paprika

After removing stems, carefully peel mushrooms. Blend together cream cheese and sour cream, add anchovy paste to taste and a sprinkling of chives and paprika. Stuff the caps (higher than the edges of the mushrooms) with the mixture. Chill. Arrange on a serving dish with fresh water cress or sprigs of parsley.

MARINATED FRESH MUSHROOMS

¼ pound medium-sized
    mushrooms
¼ teaspoon salt
¼ teaspoon dried tarragon
    or orégano (well-
    crushed)

Fresh-ground pepper
2 tablespoons wine
    vinegar (or fresh
    lemon juice)
¼ cup olive oil

Cut off half the stems, then peel mushrooms (unless snowy white) and cut them in two. Mix remaining ingredients together and add to mushrooms, tossing until all pieces are well coated. Let stand at room temperature for several hours, turning occasionally. Serve with toothpicks.

CREAM CHEESE AND RED CAVIAR

½ eight-ounce package
    cream cheese
1 tablespoon sour cream

1 teaspoon onion juice
3 ounces red caviar
Melba rounds

Combine the cream cheese, sour cream, onion juice, and *two thirds of the caviar*. Mound attractively and garnish with the balance of the caviar. Chill well before serving. Surround with Melba rounds.

ARTICHOKE HEARTS STUFFED WITH RED CAVIAR

1 ten-ounce can artichoke hearts
4 ounces red caviar

Drain artichokes and cut off small slice from bottoms so that they will stand firmly on the platter. Spoon caviar into leaves. Attractive when garnished with ripe olives.*

CURRIED ONION PARSLEY SANDWICHES

8 slices thin, white bread
2 tablespoons mayonnaise*
¼ teaspoon curry powder

2 tablespoons finely
  chopped parsley*
2 small onions, sliced very
  thin

Cut the bread with one-inch biscuit cutter to make small rounds. Blend the mayonnaise with the lemon juice and curry, and spread part of this mixture lightly on the bread rounds. Arrange onion slices on half the rounds, season with salt and cover with remaining rounds (thus making small sandwiches). Spread the balance of the mayonnaise on one side of wooden board and the chopped parsley on the other. Roll the edges of each sandwich lightly through mayonnaise (like a turning wheel) then through the parsley. Arrange on a platter, cover with nonabsorbent wrap, and chill in refrigerator until ready to serve.

CHICKEN-LIVER PATE

½ pound chicken livers
½ cup chicken broth
2 tablespoons chicken fat
2 tablespoons minced
  onion

½ teaspoon fresh lemon
  juice
2 hard-cooked eggs
Salt and fresh-ground
  pepper
Chopped parsley

Cut the chicken livers in two and simmer in chicken broth for about 10 minutes. At the same time heat *1 tablespoon fat* and slowly sauté onion until soft. Chop fine (or whirl in blender) cooked livers, *1 hard-cooked egg*, remaining 1 table-

spoon fat and lemon juice. Add salt and pepper to taste, shape
in a mound, and garnish with remaining egg, grated. Sprinkle
over lightly with chopped parsley.

If you have a helper in the kitchen (or your dinner is so
simple that you can easily return to the kitchen halfway
through cocktails to broil appetizers), I recommend the following as a grand finale to the cocktail hour. All can be made a
day ahead (except the lobster which can be prepared in the
morning) and require only a few minutes under a hot broiler
(which you can have ready and waiting).

BAKED ARTICHOKE HEARTS

These can't be beat and you can do everything the day before through "bake at 350 for 10 minutes."

1 can hearts of artichoke
Melba rye rounds (or
*   white)*
¼ pound melted butter
Salt and fresh-ground
*   pepper*

Garlic powder to taste
*   (try ¼ teaspoon)*
Slivered almonds or sesame
*   seeds*

Drain artichokes and cut in half with kitchen shears. Place
each half, *cut side up*, on a Melba round. Arrange on a copper
pan (or any other ovenproof dish on which they can be
served). In a small pan melt the butter, add salt, pepper, and
garlic powder, and spoon generously into artichoke crevices,
allowing some to run over on the rounds. Sprinkle with slivered almonds (or sesame seeds). Bake at 350 degrees for 10
minutes. Just before serving brown under hot broiler for about
3 minutes.

MARIE'S HOT CHEESE FINGERS

These, too, stop the show and can be made a day ahead.

6 slices bacon	Salt, fresh-ground pepper
½ cup thick cream sauce	Paprika
1 cup grated sharp Cheddar	Pinch dry mustard
1 small onion, grated	Shake of Worcestershire sauce
1 egg	8 slices firm white bread

Cook bacon until very crisp and drain well on paper towels. Make cream sauce and blend in grated cheese. Add finely crumbled bacon and grated onion. Beat egg and pour into mixture. Add seasonings and put aside. Cut crusts off bread slices. Toast on one side; turn, butter lightly, and toast on the other side. While warm, spread each slice generously with mixture. Dust with paprika and divide into three fingers. Place fingers on cookie tin and store in refrigerator until ready to broil. These require 3–4 minutes beneath a preheated broiler to melt and lightly brown.

BROILED STUFFED MUSHROOMS

16 mushrooms (medium-sized)	Salt and fresh-ground pepper
Olive oil (or melted butter)	1 teaspoon chopped chives (or parsley)
¼ cup finely chopped nuts	¼ teaspoon garlic powder
¼ cup fine bread crumbs	3 tablespoons light cream
	1½ tablespoons butter

Remove stems, peel the mushrooms and place them, cap side up, in a shallow, lightly-buttered casserole or copper pan. Brush the tops with oil (or melted butter) and broil for 2–3 minutes. Remove from oven and set indicator to 350 degrees. Combine remaining ingredients (*except butter*), turn the caps over and pile high with mixture. Dot well with butter and bake in 350-degree oven for 15 minutes. Put aside. When ready to serve, run under hot broiler for 3–4 minutes.

HOT LOBSTER (OR CRABMEAT) CANAPES

14 bread rounds (1½″ in diameter)
½ cup mayonnaise*
1 teaspoon fresh lemon juice
¼ teaspoon curry powder

1 cup chopped lobster or crabmeat (fresh or canned)
Grated Parmesan cheese
Paprika

Toast bread rounds on one side, remove from stove; turn, and spread lightly with a blend of mayonnaise, lemon juice, and curry powder. Cover with chopped lobster, salt to taste, and spread with balance of seasoned mayonnaise. Sprinkle each round with Parmesan cheese and a shake of paprika. Place under broiler until hot and bubbly (3–4 minutes).

Since so many appetizers call for some quantity of mayonnaise—and since homemade mayonnaise is to commercial what garden tomatoes are to winter ones—this seems a good place to insert a foolproof recipe. If you have a blender, you can make a bowl of mayonnaise in 2 minutes. It will add special flavor to salads and sandwiches as well as appetizers.

BLENDER MAYONNAISE

2 whole eggs
4 tablespoons lemon juice (or vinegar)
1 teaspoon dry mustard
1 teaspoon salt

½ teaspoon garlic powder
½ teaspoon monosodium glutamate
2 dashes cayenne pepper
2 cups salad oil

Place eggs, lemon juice, mustard, salt, garlic powder, monosodium glutamate, and cayenne pepper into the blender. *Add one half cup of the oil.* Put on cover and run blender for 5 seconds. Remove cover, turn on blender again (low speed if you have two) and slowly, but steadily, pour in the balance of the oil (1½ cups) stopping occasionally to stir with a scraper. When all the oil has been added, run the blender for a few more seconds. Correct seasoning to taste and pour into a bowl. Makes about 1 pint.

If your appetizers are delicious and accessible (your drinks ditto) the party will be off to a splendid start. I do not favor dips as they are apt to be messy and require too much exertion on the part of guests. Nuts, olives, and seasoned small crackers make a nice addition to a few more interesting appetizers. In my experience, a dish of celery curls, carrot sticks, cauliflower buds, etc., are almost as much trouble to prepare as something more delicious and usually get left at the post, especially by men. However, you know your guests, so choose what will please them.

4

Dinner is Ready

Time for dinner! Your guests probably never noticed when you slipped out of the room about ten minutes ago. Even with a well-trained helper in the kitchen, an unhurried, last-minute checkup guarantees that nothing has been forgotten or overlooked. Without a helper, there is no choice.

Don't be afraid of roasts for a dinner party. Not only are they easy to prepare and cook, but actually improve by being removed from the oven about half an hour before serving. This give the meat time to set and makes carving easier. In the case of roast beef—it gives the juices time to distribute evenly. Very little heat is lost during this time, but as a precaution, cover the roast with a blanket of aluminum foil.

Except for a few specialties such as garlic loaf* or herb bread* (that complement certain menus), I have omitted suggesting bread or rolls. At a dinner that includes potatoes or pasta and dessert, I find that few people take bread. When in doubt, I serve buttered, party rye, which is small. Again, you know your guests and will use your judgment.

Is the dinner delicious? Is it easy to prepare? Can all last-minute chores be accomplished in ten minutes? The following menus have passed these tests with honors and are planned for *dinners for six.* This is a comfortable number to entertain; most of these menus can be reduced to dinners for four (although who minds party leftovers?) and can also be expanded for eight or doubled for twelve. While seasonings, most especially salt, are not doubled—you can protect yourself by the hostess-cook theme song of "season to taste."

Menu No. 1

Entrée

Lamb Louise
Dutch noodles
Italian beans, with lemon butter
Pressed cucumbers and chives

Dessert

Mystery Torte
Coffee

LAMB LOUISE

This is the tastiest lamb and the easiest to prepare of any I know. I am never without all the necessary ingredients.

1 boned leg of lamb (about 6 pounds, reserve bones)	*1 teaspoon monosodium glutamate*
¼ pound butter (at room temperature)	*1 teaspoon salt*
1 teaspoon garlic powder	*1 teaspoon cayenne pepper*
	Fresh, chopped parsley

GRAVY

½ pint sour cream	*1 bottle capers (drained)*
¾ teaspoon saffron	*Paprika*
1 teaspoon cornstarch	

Ask your butcher to bone the lamb and include the bones in the package. On the night before your dinner party, cut off most of the fat from the lamb with a very sharp knife. Cream together butter, garlic powder, monosodium glutamate, salt, and cayenne pepper, and spread over the roast, inside and out. On a double thickness of aluminum foil, place the bones with the roast on top. Wrap tightly and *refrigerate overnight*. On the following day, remove from refrigerator 2 hours before time to roast. *Do not unwrap*. Bake, *wrapped*, in a shallow roasting pan in a 375-degree oven, allowing 35 minutes per pound for medium- or 45 minutes for well-done meat. Thirty minutes before the roast is done, remove from oven. Unwrap carefully and strain juices into a saucepan. Turn the oven up to 400 degrees, discard the bones, place the roast in the *open* aluminum foil in the pan and return to oven to brown for 30 minutes. (See *comment* at the end of this menu.)

TO MAKE THE GRAVY: To the strained lamb juice in the pan, add the sour cream and saffron. Bring to a boil, stirring constantly. Mix the cornstarch with 3 tablespoons cold water, add to mixture and boil gently for about 4 minutes. Add the drained capers and cook for a minute more, then reduce heat to lowest possible and cover gravy. (If you haven't used saffron before—it looks like short, thin threads and eventually vanishes in the gravy.) Have both lamb and gravy finished before guests arrive. Place lamb on a hot serving platter, cover with foil, and let stand. When ready to serve dinner raise the heat under gravy for a minute while you sprinkle chopped parsley over the lamb and decorate the platter with a few sprigs. Pour gravy into warmed gravy boat and sprinkle with paprika.

DUTCH NOODLES

1 eight-ounce package broad noodles	*3 tablespoons poppy seeds*
4 tablespoons butter	*2 tablespoons lemon juice*
½ cup slivered almonds	*Dash cayenne pepper*

Cook noodles according to instructions on the box. While draining, melt butter in small pan, add almonds and brown. (This goes quickly, so do not leave.) When nicely browned, add poppy seeds and lemon juice. Put noodles in the ovenproof dish in which they will be served. Pour over the butter mixture and toss gently with two forks. Sprinkle with cayenne. Cool uncovered. Dot with butter, cover with aluminum foil, and let stand. Just before guests arrive place, covered, in 400-degree oven for about 30 minutes.

ITALIAN BEANS

2 packages frozen Italian beans
3 tablespoons butter
2 tablespoons fresh lemon juice

1 teaspoon dried orégano, crushed
Salt and fresh-ground pepper

Partially thaw beans at room temperature for about an hour before cooking (they will then cook more evenly) and cook for two minutes less than the directions on the package suggest. Refresh* them under running cold water. Melt the butter, add lemon juice and orégano and pour over beans. Season with salt and pepper, toss lightly, and place in ovenproof serving dish. Leave uncovered until cool, then cover with aluminum foil. Reheat, covered, with the noodles—same temperature and same length of time.

CUCUMBERS AND CHIVES

4 long, thin cucumbers
⅔ cup white vinegar
⅓ cup salad oil
½ teaspoon sugar
1 teaspoon water
½ teaspoon salt
Fresh-ground pepper

2 tablespoons chopped chives
2 tablespoons chopped onions
1 teaspoon chopped parsley

Pare cucumbers and slice very thin. Place in a bowl, salt well, cover with wax paper on which place something heavy. Refrigerate for at least 4 hours, can be overnight. In a jar, mix together vinegar, oil, sugar, water, salt, and pepper. Press the cucumbers by holding a handful at a time between both palms and squeezing out the water. When all are limp and pressed, place in a serving bowl, add the chopped chives, and chopped onions and pour over the well-shaken salad dressing. Adjust seasoning (may not be salty enough), sprinkle with parsley, and refrigerate until time to serve.

MYSTERY TORTE

The only mystery is what makes this dessert so baffling and so delicious. Guests are forever discovering nonexistent ingredients (like dates), and a Viennese doctor once murmured nostalgically of "tortes from home." It goes from refrigerator to table without any last-minute steps and is always a success.

16 Ritz crackers
⅔ cup chopped nuts (pecans or walnuts)
3 egg whites
½ teaspoon baking
    powder } sifted together
1 cup sugar
1 teaspoon vanilla

350-DEGREE OVEN

DECORATION

½ pint whipping cream
Sugar to taste
Bitter-sweet or bitter chocolate curlicues*
    grated with vegetable parer onto whipped cream

Chop crackers and nuts together (or whirl in blender) until quite fine. Beat egg whites until stiff, gradually adding the baking-powder-sugar mixture, when whites are almost stiff. Fold in nut-cracker mixture all at once and add vanilla. Pour into lightly greased 8-inch pie plate and bake in 350-degree oven for 30 minutes. Cool.

TO PREPARE DECORATION: Whip cream, sweeten to taste, and spread over entire top of cooled torte. Garnish with chocolate shavings, or more chopped nuts. Refrigerate for at least 3 hours before serving—can be all day.

Comment:

For the purpose of this book we will assume that guests are invited to arrive at 7:15.

For this dinner, noodles, beans, cucumbers, and dessert can be comfortably prepared in the morning. Dessert first, the rest while it is baking. Time the lamb to be finished at 7:00 which means that the gravy will be made at 6:30. At that time set up the coffee. Between 7:00 and 7:15 remove lamb to serving platter and cover, take whatever appetizers you are serving to the living room, and put noodles and beans in the 400-degree oven (from whence the lamb emerged). The foil will prevent drying out. When you return to the kitchen ten minutes before serving, make the gravy piping hot, pour a little over the lamb, sprinkle with parsley. Then carry lamb, gravy boat, noodles, beans, and cucumbers to the buffet. Dessert is ready and waiting in the refrigerator. Plug in the coffee.

Menu No. 2

Entrée

Baby broilers
Tiny new potatoes in jackets, dilled
French peas and artichoke hearts
Tossed green salad
Beach plum or currant jelly

Dessert

Frieda's Chocolate Linsertorte
Coffee

BABY BROILERS

3 broilers (weighing 1¾
   to 2 pounds
   apiece, split)
½ cup olive oil
Juice of 1 large lemon
2 teaspoons dried orégano

1 teaspoon fresh-chopped
   parsley
1 clove of garlic, finely
   chopped
Salt and fresh-ground
   pepper

Wash and gently dry broilers with paper toweling. Mix together oil, lemon juice, orégano, parsley, and garlic. Place broilers (skin side up) on broiler pan; season with salt and pepper, and brush with mixture. Turn and repeat. Let stand at room temperature for two hours. When ready to cook, place 8″ below broiler heat and broil first on one side, then the other (skin side last) until browned (about 10 minutes to a side), brushing occasionally with more oil mixture. When nicely browned, pour over balance of oil mixture (add a little butter if not enough) and cover with foil. Just before guests arrive, place in preheated 375-degree oven where they can bake from 35–45 minutes, uncovered.

TINY NEW POTATOES   (in their jackets)

These are in the market during most of the year but, if not available, small peeled potato balls can be substituted.

20–24 tiny potatoes
¼ pound butter
Salt and fresh-ground
   pepper

Dried or fresh, chopped
   dill

Scrub potatoes and boil in salt water, during the morning. When almost tender, drain, then put back, uncovered, over medium heat for a minute or two, to steam until remaining moisture evaporates. Melt butter and pour over potatoes. Shake pan well until they are coated. Season with salt, pepper, and plenty of dill. Shake again, then pour into ovenproof dish. When cool, cover with aluminum foil. In the evening, heat in the same oven, covered, with the baking broilers.

FRENCH PEAS AND ARTICHOKES

Seldom are vegetables so easy to prepare or so delicious to eat.

⅛ pound butter
2 tablespoons frozen
   chopped onion
2 cans artichoke hearts
   (*drained*)

2 cans petits pois
   (*drained*)
Salt and fresh-ground
   pepper

Melt butter in a saucepan and pare frozen chopped onions into pan. Let cook over low heat for about 3 minutes, then add artichokes and turn gently to coat with butter-onion mixture. Butter a shallow casserole (from which the vegetables will be served) and make a bed of the peas. Spoon over the artichokes and any drippings from the pan. If not enough butter, dot with a little more. Cool, then cover with aluminum foil. In the evening, place in oven, covered, with broilers and potatoes.

TOSSED GREEN SALAD

2 or 3 different kinds of
   greens (Bibb, iceberg,
   romaine, endive, etc.)
1 hard-cooked egg

Fresh or dried herbs
French dressing
*Chopped parsley**

In the morning, while egg is cooking, wash and thoroughly dry the salad greens, separating leaves (Bibb), and tearing iceberg into pieces with fingers. Place a paper towel in the bottom of a cellophane bag and fill with greens. Cut up any available fresh herbs (chives, dill, lovage, tarragon, etc.) and place in wax paper. Grate egg and place in wax paper and deposit both next to the bag of greens, in the refrigerator.

Place, conveniently at hand, wooden salad bowl, French dressing, and chopped parsley, so that assembling and tossing the salad in the evening will take only about 2 minutes.

TART FRENCH DRESSING

½ cup oil (your choice)
¼ cup wine vinegar
1 teaspoon salt
½ teaspoon fresh-ground pepper
¼ teaspoon sugar

½ teaspoon dry mustard
1 teaspoon Worcestershire sauce
2 teaspoons lemon juice
1 teaspoon water
Slit garlic bud in bottle

Mix all the ingredients in a jar with screw-on top. Add garlic bud. Shake well before using. Put greens in bowl, salt lightly, and toss with enough dressing to lightly coat but leaving no excess liquid in the bottom of the bowl.

FRIEDA'S CHOCOLATE LINSERTORTE

This dessert is *better* if made the day before and iced on the day of serving.

2 cups ground unblanched almonds
¼ pound butter (at room temperature)
1½ cups sugar

2 eggs
¼ cup all-purpose flour
1 teaspoon vanilla
Medium-sized springform

325-DEGREE OVEN

ICING

½ cup dark-brown sugar (packed down firmly)
½ cup white sugar
½ cup evaporated milk

1 teaspoon white corn syrup
1½ ounces bitter chocolate
1 teaspoon vanilla

TO PREPARE TORTE: Grind almonds (using coarse blade of meat grinder or blender). For this, and all other desserts, I use the electric mixer for every step possible (with the exception of whipping cream which I feel safer doing by hand). Cream the butter, add sugar gradually, and beat until light and creamy. Add the eggs—*one at a time*—beating after each addition. Mix together flour and almonds and stir, all at once, into mixture. Add vanilla, and pour into buttered, lightly floured, 8-inch springform. Bake in 325-degree oven *for 15 minutes*, then increase heat to 350 degrees and bake 35–40 minutes more (or until torte is a medium brown).

TO PREPARE ICING: Cook together all the ingredients, *except vanilla*, until the mixture forms a soft ball. Add vanilla, beat for a minute or two off the stove, then ice the torte. Cool. Place in refrigerator for at least 4 hours before serving (can be longer) so that icing will be firm.

Comment:

Everything can be prepared for this dinner in the morning except the broilers (which can be ready to go into the oven) and the salad (which is ready to toss). Suggest broiling the chickens at 6:30, occasionally basting and meanwhile setting up coffee and attending to any other unfinished business such as appetizers, bread, etc. Just before guests arrive, place chickens, potatoes, and vegetables (all covered by foil, which can be used over and over again) into a 375-degree oven together. Ten minutes before serving, return to kitchen to baste broilers, arrange on warm serving platter and quickly cut off ends of drumsticks with kitchen shears (this step takes only a minute and adds enormously to their appearance. I also snip off the wing tips). Next, toss salad, sprinkle chopped parsley wherever indicated and bring everything to the buffet.

Menu No. 3

Entrée

Baked glazed ham
Lyonnaise potatoes
Chived, creamed spinach

Herb cole slaw with tomato strips
Buttered party rye
Mustard pickles

Dessert

Crustless apple pie
Brandied hard sauce
Coffee

BAKED GLAZED HAM

*5-pound canned ham
(You will have
leftovers but what
could be nicer?)
Dark-brown sugar
Barbecue sauce
(any brand)*

*1 cup Madeira (or other
sweet wine)
Cognac
Orange marmalade
1 cup water (if needed)*

TO PREPARE HAM: Score ham on fat side (about ½″ deep) and cover top with brown sugar, then barbecue sauce. Sprinkle over a little of the Madeira and pour the rest in the pan. Follow baking instructions on the can; 30 minutes before the ham is finished, remove from oven, add more brown sugar, lather generously with orange marmalade, and pour over a few tablespoons of cognac. If necessary, add water to pan and return to oven. When finished cooking, place on oven-proof serving platter, cover loosely with foil, and reduce heat to 225 degrees. Return ham to slow oven just before guests arrive.

TO PREPARE GRAVY: Place pan in which ham baked over heat on top of stove. Scrape well and add a little more Madeira. Serve either strained or not.

LYONNAISE POTATOES

These can be timed to be finished just before guests arrive and then put under the broiler before being served to heat quickly.

3 tablespoons butter
1 tablespoon salad oil
2 tablespoons chopped frozen onion
3 cups boiled, cubed potatoes

Salt and fresh-ground pepper
¼ cup beef consommé
Chopped parsley

Melt butter and oil in skillet, add onion and cook slowly until soft, not browned. Add potatoes and seasonings and gently mix well. Add consommé and cover pan. Cook slowly until potato is brown underneath (about 30 minutes). Fold in two (like an omelet) and transfer to ovenproof serving dish. Let stand, covered by foil, in warm oven with ham. Place under hot broiler for about three minutes before serving.

CHIVED, CREAMED SPINACH

3 ten-ounce packages frozen, chopped spinach (this may seem like a lot, but there is never a drop left)
½ cup water
½ teaspoon salt

3 ounces chived, cream cheese (can be purchased this way or add your own fresh, chopped chives to cream cheese)
½ teaspoon garlic powder
½ cup cream
1 hard-cooked egg

Boil water, add salt and spinach and cook until spinach is just defrosted. Drain well, return to pan, add chived cheese and garlic powder and stir over low heat until cheese is melted and blended. Whirl in blender with cream for 1 minute (or chop fine in a bowl). Adjust seasoning and pour into top of double boiler. Grate egg and store it in refrigerator. Place spinach over heat just before guests arrive.

HERB COLE SLAW

1 teaspoon salt
½ teaspoon fresh-ground pepper
½ teaspoon dry mustard
½ teaspoon caraway seeds
1 teaspoon celery salt
1–2 tablespoons sugar (start with 1, add more if needed)
3 tablespoons salad oil
½ cup vinegar
1½ tablespoons finely chopped pimento

1 teaspoon pared frozen, chopped onion
1 teaspoon mixed dried herbs (dill, tarragon, etc.) or straight salad mixture
1 medium-sized cabbage, shredded
½ green pepper, shredded (optional)
1 ripe red tomato, concassed*
Chopped, fresh parsley

Mix together seasonings, oil and vinegar. Place cabbage and pepper in a separate bowl and lightly toss in well-blended dressing. Arrange on serving dish. Put *concassed* tomato in remaining dressing, then use to decorate slaw. Sprinkle with parsley and refrigerate until ready to serve.

CRUSTLESS APPLE PIE

4 pounds tart green apples
1½ cups brown sugar
Juice of ½ lemon
2 tablespoons brandy

Pinch of cinnamon (about ⅛ teaspoon)
¼ pound butter
1 cup flour
Pinch of salt

350-DEGREE OVEN

TO PREPARE PIE: Pare and slice apples into a large bowl. Add *one half of the brown sugar*, lemon juice, brandy and cinnamon. Mix thoroughly and let stand for about 15 minutes. Meanwhile lightly butter an 8-inch pie plate. In a bowl mix together (with fingers) butter, flour, salt, and balance of brown sugar (¾ cup). Arrange apples in pie plate and sprinkle this mixture over the entire top, pressing down firmly around the edges. Bake in a 350-degree oven for 1 hour.

BRANDIED HARD SAUCE

¼ *pound butter (at room*   *2 tablespoons brandy (or*
   temperature)   *2 tablespoons sherry,*
1 cup confectioners' sugar   *or 1 teaspoon vanilla)*
½ *teaspoon lemon juice*

Cream butter, add sugar and flavoring. Pile lightly in a serving bowl and swirl the top into a peak. Refrigerate until two hours before serving, then let stand at room temperature. Can be made the day before.

Comment:

By the time guests arrive, ham is waiting in warm oven; potatoes are cooked and need only a few minutes under broiler, just before being served; spinach is heating in top of double boiler; salad and dessert are finished business. Rye can be buttered well ahead and left in basket under nonabsorbent wrap, pickles can be arranged on serving dish and left in refrigerator. During ten minutes before serving, transfer spinach and potatoes to warm serving plate, sprinkle grated egg on spinach, plug in coffee, and carry food to buffet.

Menu No. 4

Entrée

Sauerbraten
Noodles and cheese
Glazed onions and carrots
Green salad with herb mayonnaise

Dessert

Gâteau Ganache
Coffee

SAUERBRATEN

4-pound eye of the round   Salt and fresh-ground
3 tablespoons flour   pepper
                                                  3 tablespoons fat

MARINADE

1½ cups of vinegar   3 bay leaves
½ cup Burgundy (or   3 big onions sliced
    other red, dry wine)   12 whole cloves
1 cup water   2 teaspoons salt
10 peppercorns   1 teaspoon mustard seed
2 tablespoons sugar

GRAVY

Strained pan juices
4 ground ginger snaps
Balance of marinade

From 2–4 days before the dinner (the longer the better), combine all marinade ingredients. Place meat in a large, shallow bowl and pour over the marinade. Store in refrigerator, turning two or three times a day.

TO PREPARE SAUERBRATEN: Remove from refrigerator at least two hours before cooking. Strain the marinade into a pan and reserve onions. Dry meat well with paper toweling, season the flour with salt and pepper, and coat meat on all sides. Heat fat in Dutch oven or roasting pan on top of the stove until very hot, then brown meat on all sides until a dark brown. Pour *half* the marinade over the meat, add the reserved onions, cover tightly, and simmer 3½–4 hours (or until tender). Remove meat to a platter, cover with aluminum foil, and strain pan juices into a wide-mouth jar or bowl. This can be done in the morning (or even the day before), thus giving the fat in the gravy time to surface in the refrigerator and hence easy to remove. The gravy can be made at your convenience and the meat improves by cooking twice.

TO PREPARE GRAVY: Remove fat from top of pan juices and pour into small saucepan. Cook over medium heat and when hot add the ginger snaps and balance of marinade. Adjust the seasoning, and thicken slightly (1–2 tablespoons flour mixed with a little cold water) if desired. Cover and leave on stove to be reheated later.

About fifteen minutes before guests arrive, put meat back in Dutch oven, pour over some of the gravy (about half a cup), cover and simmer over low heat until ready to serve.

NOODLES AND CHEESE

1 eight-ounce package   ½ cup grated sharp
    broad noodles   Cheddar
¼ pound butter   Grated Parmesan
                                Paprika

Have at least 4 quarts of salted water (1 teaspoon salt per quart of water) boiling briskly before adding noodles. Cook until barely tender (about 8 minutes) and drain. Melt butter. Pour noodles into ovenproof casserole and pour over melted butter and Cheddar. Toss well (with fork and spoon) until well coated. Shake Parmesan lightly over top, sprinkle with paprika, add a few extra dots of butter and let stand. When ready to reheat, cover and put into 375-degree oven for about 30–40 minutes.

GLAZED CARROTS

1 package winter carrots   Salt
2 tablespoons butter   Chopped parsley
2 teaspoons sugar

Peel carrots with vegetable parer, then cut into chunks about 1¼" long. Round out cut edges with parer, so that chunks resemble bullets. Place them in a deep saucepan, barely cover with water, add butter, sugar, and salt, and bring to a boil. Reduce heat to medium, cover pan, and cook for 15 minutes. Remove cover, turn heat up high as possible. In about 10 minutes (keep your eye on the pan) the liquid will evaporate and the butter and sugar will blend to form a glaze. Shake the pan so that all the carrots (now a beautiful, bright orange) will be coated with the glaze. Pour into a serving dish (a double, if you have one) and let cool. Onions will occupy other half of dish.

GLAZED ONIONS

1 tablespoon butter
2 tablespoons drippings
   from sauerbraten

2 cans boiled, white
   onions
1 teaspoon sugar
Paprika

Heat butter and drippings in a skillet and add onions. Coat well by turning gently, at the same time sprinkling with sugar and paprika. Cook, uncovered, over *very* slow heat until slightly browned and glazed (about 1 hour). Turn occasionally. When done, pour into same double dish or platter with carrots.

GREEN SALAD WITH HERB MAYONNAISE

2 or 3 varieties of salad
   greens, washed and
   thoroughly dried
1 cup mayonnaise*
1 teaspoon finely chopped
   chives

1 teaspoon finely chopped
   dill
1 teaspoon finely chopped
   tarragon leaves
2 tablespoons fresh,
   chopped parsley*

Arrange washed and dried greens in salad bowl (lined with paper toweling which can be yanked out) in refrigerator. Fold chives, dill, and tarragon into mayonnaise and chill for a few hours. *Dried herbs may be substituted, using one half the quantities.* Just before serving toss the salad well and, at that time, add the parsley, both throughout the salad and over the top.

GATEAU GANACHE

When I ask my husband to suggest a company dessert, he says "gâteau ganache" without a moment's hesitation.

6 egg whites

12 ounces sugar

6 ounces ground nuts
  (pecans or walnuts)

1½ teaspoons white wine
  vinegar

½ teaspoon vanilla

(1 sheet parchment
  paper)

375-DEGREE OVEN

FILLING AND ICING

3 ounces semisweet chocolate

½ pint whipping cream

What is coming now looks complicated—please take my word for the fact that you will never make an easier nor more rewarding dessert. Up to "filling and icing" you can make this two or three days ahead, as long as you keep it in a tightly closed tin. Here we go:

Place egg whites in large mixing bowl and let stand an hour or so at room temperature. Prepare two 8-inch cake tins as follows: Cut two rounds of parchment paper to fit bottom of pan (use a pencil, stand pan on paper, run pencil around bottom of edge, and cut out. Get your man to cut out a dozen at a time—mine does). Grease and lightly flour cake tins (bottom and sides), cover bottom with fitted paper, grease and lightly flour paper. (You can do this faster than I can tell you how.)

Beat egg whites until stiff. Add sugar and nuts, all at once, and fold in gently with a metal spoon. Add vinegar and vanilla, and spoon lightly into prepared tins. Put in 375-degree oven and bake for 35–40 minutes (or until crusty to the touch). Have two wire cakeracks ready. Run a knife around the edges, cover with racks (*turned upside down*), and quickly turn over so that meringues rest on racks. Remove tins and, at once, peel off the parchment paper. So much for *that* day.

PREPARE FILLING AND ICING: On the day of dinner, at your convenience:

Melt the chocolate in double boiler (or small pan over hot water) and while cooling, whip cream until very stiff. Put *half of the cream* in a separate bowl and add *half the chocolate*. Place one meringue round on serving platter and cover with this mixture. Top with second meringue. Cover this one with balance of whipped cream. With a spatula, dip into chocolate and make swirls on the whipped cream, so that it has a marbled effect. (Don't worry, whatever you do will look fine.) Use plenty of chocolate, it will harden and add a lot of interest and deliciousness. Grate a little bitter or semi-sweet chocolate over the top and prepare for applause. Store dessert in refrigerator until ready to serve. (I always put wax paper on the shelf above as insurance against anything dripping onto it.)

Comment:

Just before guests arrive, turn on heat beneath sauerbraten and put noodles, carrots, and onions (all covered with foil) in 375-degree oven. Ten minutes before serving, heat gravy, toss salad and sprinkle with parsley, put meat on platter, pour over a few tablespoons of gravy, and sprinkle with parsley, and carry them plus noodles, carrots, and onions (sprinkled with parsley and paprika respectively) to buffet.

Menu No. 5

Entrée

Lobster Maggie
Baked stuffed potatoes
Vegetable salad platter
Garlic loaf

Dessert

Crème Brulée
Coffee

LOBSTER MAGGIE

6 one and a half pound
    lobsters (split live—
    your fishmonger will
    split them for you)
Olive oil
Tomalley and coral from
    the lobsters
2 cups cracker crumbs
    (or fine bread
    crumbs)

½ pound melted butter
¼ cup fresh lemon juice
1 teaspoon Worcestershire
    sauce
Salt and fresh-ground
    pepper
Fresh-chopped parsley
    and chives (or 1
    teaspoon each, dried)
12 lemon wedges

BUTTER SAUCE

½ pound butter

To prepare lobsters—mix together in a bowl all ingredients and adjust seasoning to taste. Brush lobsters thoroughly, *inside and out*, with oil. Stuff lobsters lightly with mixture and arrange on foil-lined, closed cookie tin. They can now remain in the refrigerator until ready to cook. Before guests arrive, preheat oven to 500 degrees, and place lobsters at room temperature. A few minutes after guests arrive, return to kitchen long enough to put lobsters in the oven where they must bake for exactly 25 minutes. Time them so that once done, they can be served at once. Have quartered lemons* ready in refrigerator.

TO PREPARE BUTTER SAUCE: Put the butter in the top of a double boiler over simmering water and allow butter to melt without stirring. The clear butter will rise to the surface while the sediment remains at the bottom. When ready to serve, pour gently into individual sauce dishes, to accompany the lobsters.

BAKED STUFFED POTATOES

6 medium-to-large firm, mature potatoes. (If you have a freezer, double quantity and freeze half)
¼ cup hot milk
⅛ pound butter

Salt and fresh-ground pepper
½ small onion, grated
1 egg
Parmesan cheese
Paprika

Bake potatoes at any convenient temperature from 350 to 425 degrees until soft (you might be doing them the day before and cooking something else at the same time). Cut in two lengthwise, and scoop out insides into a big bowl (or electric mixing bowl). Beat well, adding milk, until mixture is soft, fluffy, and smooth. Add seasoning, onion, and egg, mix well, and fill shells generously. Sprinkle lightly with Parmesan cheese and paprika. Arrange on an open roasting pan about 2 inches deep. Cool. Cover with aluminum foil and refrigerate. Reheat at the same time and in the same oven as the lobsters.

SALAD DRESSING

½ teaspoon dried dill
½ teaspoon dried tarragon
½ teaspoon salt

½ teaspoon fresh-ground pepper
½ teaspoon dry mustard
½ cup salad oil
¼ cup lemon juice

Place all the ingredients in a jar with a screw-on top. Shake well when mixing, and again before using.

VEGETABLE-SALAD PLATTER

2–3 *small heads of lettuce*   1 *can tiny whole string*
2 *cans green asparagus*   *beans*
        spears   1 *can tiny whole beets*
                                         Fresh, chopped parsley

After washing and drying, break up lettuce with the fingers and place in a wooden salad bowl, lined with paper toweling. Drain asparagus, beans, and beets, place in separate bowls, marinate lightly in salad dressing, and refrigerate.

GARLIC LOAF

1 *loaf unsliced white bread*
¼ *pound butter (at room temperature)*
¼–½ *teaspoon garlic powder*

Remove *all* crust from the bread and cut into thick slices not quite through to the bottom (being careful to keep the loaf together). Blend together butter and garlic powder and spread the mixture on both sides of each slice. Then cut loaf into thirds the long way, again not cutting quite through to the bottom and keeping the loaf together. Wrap in a double thickness of brown paper (used bags come in handy for this) and tie with a string as though ready to mail. Place in a 400-degree oven for 20 minutes (before lobsters go in) and keep wrapped until ready to serve. Place, intact, in a basket so that guests can break off their own pieces. Especially good with lobster!

CREME BRULEE

Easy to make and easy to eat. Invite your guest of honor, or one of your guests, to lightly tap the glazed surface with the back of a silver serving spoon.

1 *quart whipping cream*   2 *teaspoons vanilla*
2 *tablespoons sugar*   *Soft*, light-brown *sugar*
8 *egg yolks*

                                    325-DEGREE OVEN

Heat the cream in the top of a double boiler until hot, but not scalding. Add sugar and stir until dissolved. Beat egg yolks in a separate bowl until well blended; then add to mixture with vanilla. Pour into a shallow, rectangular, Pyrex dish (13½″ by 8½″ by 1½″) and place in a pan containing a few inches of hot water. Bake in a 325-degree oven for 1 hour (or until set—insert a silver knife to test). Cool and place dish in refrigerator for several hours. (This much can be done the day before or first thing in the morning.) A few hours before serving, remove from refrigerator and cover entire surface with a quarter of an inch of sifted, light-brown sugar. Turn on broiler and, when blazing hot, place dish 4 inches beneath heat. *Seat yourself in front of the open oven door and don't take your eyes off the dessert.* In a minute or two the sugar will begin to melt in beads and soon the entire top will be glazed and shiny. Leave in oven until the whole surface looks melted, and tiny wisps of smoke start coming up—then remove at once and cool. (This oven procedure will take only 4–5 minutes.) When cool, return to refrigerator until ready to serve (best if icy cold). The glaze cracks with a light tap, and your only problem will be—have you enough for seconds?

Comment:

Before guests arrive, bake garlic loaf, and then preheat the oven to 500 degrees. Shortly after all guests are present, return to the kitchen long enough to put lobsters and potatoes in oven (for 25 minutes). Ten minutes before serving, toss salad and arrange vegetables, and sprinkle all with parsley; unwrap garlic loaf, put lobsters, potatoes, and lemons on large platter, and bring everything to the buffet.

Menu No. 6

Entrée

Casserole of stuffed veal chops with mushrooms
Baked potato slices
Dilled green beans
Artichoke salad with concassed tomatoes

Dessert

Chocolate Mousse Basque
Coffee

CASSEROLE OF STUFFED VEAL CHOPS

4 ounces butter
1 small onion
6 large kidney veal chops,
    1¼ inches thick
12 medium-to-large
    mushrooms
2 tablespoons lemon juice
Salt and fresh-ground
    pepper

Chopped parsley
1 cup chicken stock
    (or canned broth)
½ cup red wine
1 can pâté de foie gras
Toothpicks or small
    skewers

350-DEGREE OVEN

Melt the butter in a large, heavy skillet. Grate the juice and pulp of the onion into the pan, blend well over moderate heat. Add chops and brown on both sides until very dark. Set aside on a platter.

Peel mushroom caps (unwashed), remove stems and slice thinly. In the same skillet (unwashed), add a little more butter, lemon juice, salt, pepper, and parsley, and sauté the mushrooms *and* sliced stems over quite high heat for about 4 minutes. Remove the caps to a dish, then add stock to pan and blend with remaining juices and mushroom stems. Add wine and let simmer, over very low heat, while stuffing the chops.

Using a small, sharp knife, cut a pocket down the center of the fat end of the cooled veal chop—about ½ inch away from either end and cut right down to the bone. Make the pocket about 2 inches long and fill slit (which will gape open) with about 1 teaspoon *pâté* apiece. Hold together with toothpicks (or small skewers). Arrange the chops in the ovenproof dish in which they will be served and pour over them the contents of the skillet. (This much can be done in the morning.) About 15 minutes before guests are due, place in a 350-degree oven to bake for 40 minutes. (This is the minimum time required, but if guests are late and chops bake an extra 15–20 minutes, it will do no harm.)

BAKED POTATO SLICES

These are different, delicious, and seldom seen.

6–8 medium-sized, long potatoes	*Salt and fresh-ground pepper*
Butter	*Paprika*
	4 ounces melted butter

Scrub potatoes and rub them with butter. *Do not peel.* Cut them into ¼" slices (the narrow way). Place them in a well-buttered ovenproof serving dish (or iron skillet). Season with salt, pepper, sprinkle with paprika, and pour over melted butter. Cover with aluminum foil and bake in oven with veal chops—same temperature, same length of time.

DILLED GREEN BEANS

2 packages frozen,
    frenched string beans
½ cup chicken stock

1 teaspoon minced onion
1 tablespoon butter
Salt to taste

SAUCE

2 tablespoons butter
½ cup sour cream
2 teaspoons fresh-chopped
    (or 1 teaspoon dried)
    dill

Salt and fresh-ground
    pepper

Partially thaw the beans before cooking. Bring stock, onion, and butter to a boil, add salt and beans. Cover and cook over medium heat for 3 minutes. Pour into a strainer and refresh.* Spread in one layer on a large platter so that beans will cool quickly. When cool, melt butter, add sour cream, dill, and seasonings. Place beans in ovenproof serving dish and pour over sauce. Cover with foil. Put in oven (at the same time with chops and potatoes).

ARTICHOKE SALAD

2 cans artichoke hearts
2 concassed tomatoes*
1-2 heads lettuce

Salad dressing*
Fresh or dried herbs to
    taste

Drain artichokes and concass tomatoes. Wash and dry lettuce and put in wooden bowl lined with paper toweling. Refrigerate. Make salad dressing and marinate drained artichokes and tomatoes (in separate bowls). Use your choice of herbs (chives are very good with artichokes—so are most others). Refrigerate next to salad bowl.

CHOCOLATE MOUSSE BASQUE

This recipe will fill 10 three-inch individual fluted, white soufflé dishes or a seven-inch large one.

12 ounces semisweet   *6 eggs, separated*
    chocolate (the better   *2 tablespoons rum or*
    the quality, the better   *kirsch (more, if you*
    the mousse)   *like)*
5 ounces black coffee   *½ pint whipping cream*
1 ounce butter

Melt the chocolate in the coffee and cook to a thick cream, stirring constantly (about 2–3 minutes). Remove from fire and beat in the butter. When melted, add the egg yolks, ONE BY ONE. Add rum (or kirsch). Beat egg whites until very stiff and stir briskly into mixture with a metal spoon. When thoroughly blended, taste to decide whether you want a little more liquor, then pour into soufflé dish. Refrigerate overnight, if possible, surely for 6 hours. Whip cream, sweeten to taste, cover tightly and refrigerate. When convenient in late afternoon, spoon or pipe whipped cream around or over the top. Pare a little bitter (or semisweet chocolate) over the whipped-cream surface and leave in refrigerator until ready to serve.

Comment:

Ten minutes before serving dinner, put mushrooms in a pan over medium heat; turn potato slices and add a little more butter, if necessary; toss the salad and spread artichokes and tomato across the top. Sprinkle with parsley. Bring everything to the table.

Menu No. 7

Entrée

Tournedos with mushroom sauce
Château potatoes
Baked stuffed tomatoes
Tossed salad with Roquefort dressing

Dessert

Fruit Mélange and sour cream
Coffee

TOURNEDOS

Steak is probably more popular than any other meat, certainly with men, and about the easiest to prepare. However, it does not make for relaxed-hostess cooking because the minute you turn your back it becomes well done. Tournedos solve the problem and this meal is planned so that although they will consume most of that last ten minutes, almost nothing else will need attention.

6 Tournedos
(Filet steaks about 1
inch thick and 2½
inches in diameter,
wrapped in very thin
strips of bacon tied
on with a string—your
butcher will do this)

2 tablespoons butter
1 tablespoon oil
Salt and fresh-ground
*   pepper*
½ cup stock (or canned
*   bouillon)*
¼ cup Madeira

MUSHROOM SAUCE

½ pound fresh
mushrooms, sliced or
whole
2 tablespoons butter
1 tablespoon oil

1 tablespoon chopped,
frozen onions
Salt and fresh-ground
pepper

Place tournedos in marinade* at room temperature, a few hours before cooking.

TO PREPARE MUSHROOMS: In the morning heat butter and oil, add onions and sauté for 5 minutes. Add mushrooms and cook slowly for 5 minutes more. Season and set aside until evening.

See "Comment" for balance of cooking instructions.

CHATEAU POTATOES

6 medium-sized potatoes,
pared, quartered, and
edges rounded with
vegetable parer

Salt and fresh-ground
pepper
⅛ pound butter
2 tablespoons oil
Chopped parsley

After shaping potatoes, soak in cold water for a few minutes. Dry thoroughly, season with salt and pepper. Heat butter and oil in skillet, add potatoes, and sauté very slowly until they are nicely browned and very soft. Put aside to reheat just before serving.

BAKED STUFFED TOMATOES

6 firm, ripe, red tomatoes
Salt and fresh-ground pepper

STUFFING

½ cup fine bread crumbs	*3 tablespoons frozen,*
¼ cup olive oil	*chopped onion*
1 clove of garlic, mashed	*3 tablespoons fresh,*
¼ teaspoon thyme	*chopped parsley*
¼ teaspoon salt	*Fresh-ground pepper*

TO PREPARE THE TOMATOES: Remove stems and cut into halves, crosswise. Press out the juice and seeds. Cut small sliver from bottoms so that they will stand straight. Cover each half with a large spoonful of stuffing. Sprinkle with a few drops of oil and arrange on a shallow, lightly oiled, ovenproof serving dish. Put aside until evening.

TO PREPARE STUFFING: Mix together all ingredients in a bowl, correct seasoning to taste.

TOSSED GREEN SALAD

2 small heads different varieties of lettuce, endive, ro-
maine, etc., if in season
Chopped chives
Chopped parsley

ROQUEFORT CHEESE DRESSING

¼ pound Roquefort	*½ teaspoon dry mustard*
cheese	*½ tablespoon*
6 tablespoons salad oil	*Worcestershire sauce*
3 tablespoons lemon juice	*Salt*
¼ teaspoon paprika	

Wash and dry greens, place herbs in wax paper, deposit greens in salad bowl (lined with paper toweling), and place herb package on top. Refrigerate.

TO MAKE DRESSING: Grate cheese into a bowl. Add oil slowly, stirring with small wire whisk. Add remaining ingredients and stir until well blended. Leave at room temperature and stir well before tossing salad just before serving dinner.

FRUIT MELANGE

12 macaroons, crumbled (they can be bought by the pound this way)
4 cups canned fruit (drained freestone peach halves, pineapple spears, apricot halves, Bing cherries, etc.)

½ cup almonds, slivered, and toasted in a little butter (can be bought slivered in supermarkets)
¼ cup dark-brown sugar
¼ cup sherry

350-DEGREE OVEN

SAUCE

1 pint sour cream
1 tablespoon sugar
Pinch of cinnamon

TO PREPARE FRUIT: Butter a 2-quart casserole and cover bottom with some of the macaroon crumbs. Add a layer of mixed fruit, then continue alternating fruit and crumbs, ending with crumbs. Sprinkle toasted almonds and brown sugar over the top, then dribble over with sherry. Bake in a 350-degree oven for 35 minutes. Turn off heat and let casserole remain in oven for another 20 minutes.

Serve at room temperature accompanied by a bowl of sour cream blended with sugar and garnished with a pinch of cinnamon.

Comment:

Before guests arrive, pat tournedos dry so that they are ready to be sautéed and preheat oven to 400 degrees for tomatoes and potatoes. On your return, put tomatoes and potatoes in oven and after heating butter and oil in skillet, sauté steaks 3–4 minutes to a side. While steaks are cooking, toss the salad. When steaks are done, remove to warm platter and cut off strings. Pour fat out of skillet and stir in bouillon and Madeira. Boil quickly over high heat (scraping sides of pan) for a minute or two, then add mushrooms, blend well, and pour hot mushroom sauce over steaks. Sprinkle with parsley, surround with baked tomatoes, and carry everything to the table.

Menu No. 8

Entrée

Breast of chicken Patsy
Hashed brown potatoes
Fresh asparagus, with lemon butter
Mushroom, celery, tomato salad
Beach plum or currant jelly

Dessert

Soufflé Monte Cristo
Coffee

BREAST OF CHICKEN PATSY

3 chicken breasts, split in two
1 quart milk
Salt and fresh-ground pepper
1 cup flour
1 teaspoon seasoned salt

1 cup chicken broth
½ teaspoon fresh-ground pepper
½ teaspoon paprika
1 tablespoon mixed herbs (dried)
Vegetable shortening

400-DEGREE OVEN

Put chicken in large bowl, cover with milk, and season with salt and pepper. Let stand at least 1 hour. In a brown-paper bag put flour, seasoned salt, pepper, paprika, and herbs. Mix well. Dry chicken breasts on paper toweling, and place, two at a time, in bag. Coat well with flour, remove from bag and shake off excess flour. Heat heavy skillet, add vegetable shortening to a depth of 1½ inches and fry, skin side down, until very brown. Turn and fry other side. When well browned put in roasting pan and repeat until all pieces are browned. Add chicken broth and place roaster, *covered*, in a 400-degree oven and bake for 15 minutes. Reduce heat to 325 and bake for 40 minutes more. Remove cover for last 10 minutes before serving, then arrange on hot platter with bunches of parsley or cress at either end. *No gravy*—this chicken is crisp on the outside, and juicy and delicious inside.

HASHED BROWN POTATOES

6 *medium-sized potatoes*	2 *tablespoons bacon fat*
2 *tablespoons chopped,*	(*or whatever*
frozen onion	*preferred*)
Salt and fresh-ground	*Chopped parsley*
pepper	

do not
refrig.

Boil potatoes, with skins on, in salted water until almost tender. Let cool; peel and dice. Add chopped onion to bowl and mix lightly. Season. Melt fat in iron skillet and sauté potatoes until well done on all sides. Pour into buttered ovenproof dish and let cool, uncovered. Let stand until evening. Reheat in 400° oven 15-20 min. before serving.

FRESH ASPARAGUS

2 *pounds asparagus*	*Juice of 2 lemons*
⅛ *pound butter*	*Salt*

Scrape stalks of asparagus, snap off tough ends with fingers (at nearest breaking point) and wash well. Tie in small bunches and stand in ½ inch cold water until ready to cook.

do not refrig

Place in enamel asparagus pan, cover with boiling, salted water; and cook over high heat, uncovered, for about 10 minutes, or until tender. Pour carefully into collander, refresh* with cold water, drain well, and place in ovenproof serving dish, uncovered. Set aside until evening. *Reheat in 400° oven 15-20 min. before serving.*

SALAD

12 *mushrooms, peeled*
(*if medium-sized, cut
in half, if larger,
quarter*)
4 *stalks white celery, cut
into pieces the size of
large matches cut in
two*
½ *green pepper* (*cut into
Julienne strips*)
1 *tablespoon minced
onion* (*chop the
frozen very fine*)
French dressing*
2 *heads lettuce* (Bibb *if
possible*)
1 *red tomato*, concassed
Fresh, *chopped parsley*
Salt *and* fresh-ground
pepper

On the day before the dinner, mix mushrooms, celery, green pepper, and onion in a bowl, spoon over 2–3 tablespoons French dressing and turn until vegetables are lightly coated. Leave in refrigerator, turning occasionally, until ready to use. On removing from refrigerator, season with salt and pepper. On the day of the party, thoroughly wash the Bibb lettuce, dry and put in paper-lined salad bowl. Place the *concassed* tomato* in wax paper on top of the bowl next to the marinating vegetables, so that everything will be at hand for quick assembling just before dinner.

SOUFFLE MONTE CRISTO

This unusual and elegant dessert can be made the day before, except for a small whipped-cream decoration, and the cream can be whipped and added any convenient time on *the* day. Looks hard—but isn't. You only have to do one step at a time and it requires no cooking.

4 egg yolks	½ cup semisweet, pared,
3 egg whites	chocolate curlicues
3 ounces very fine	7-inch soufflé dish
granulated sugar	(or equivalent)
1 pint milk	4 macaroons, broken into
1 envelope gelatine	small pieces
Split vanilla pod (or	1–2 tablespoons rum
1 teaspoon extract)	(or Kirsch)
5 ounces whipping cream	

DECORATION

3 ounces whipping cream (whipped stiff)
Some of above pared chocolate

Separate eggs, putting whites in mixing bowl and yolks in top of double boiler. Measure sugar onto wax paper, combine milk and vanilla. (If using vanilla bean instead of extract— bring to just under a boil.) Make a custard by blending yolks, sugar, and milk, and cook over moderate heat until mixture thickens enough to coat back of spoon. Remove pan at once from stove and strain custard into a bowl. Place bowl in a large pan (or ice bucket) filled with ice. Dissolve gelatin in 2–3 tablespoons water in a small, *enamel* pan (or stainless steel one—aluminum turns it black) and then heat on stove until *hot*. Add to mixture, stirring briskly with whisk and keep on stirring until mixture is on the point of thickening (about 10 minutes) Beat 5 ounces of cream until *one half stiff.* Beat egg whites until stiff and shiny, but not dry. Fold into mixture—cream, first; whites, second. Pour a layer of mixture into soufflé dish, sprinkle over with chocolate, and repeat, ending with soufflé on top, and reserving a little of the chocolate for later decoration. Place an empty glass in the center of the dish and fill the glass with ice cubes to hold it down. Place dish in refrigerator and let soufflé set. Break up macaroon pieces and soak in rum. When soufflé is set, gently remove the glass and fill the cavity with macaroon pieces. Return to refrigerator.

TO PREPARE DECORATION: On the day of the dinner (anytime) whip remaining 3 ounces of cream, sweeten to taste, and pipe or spoon around edge. Sprinkle with balance of chocolate over the top. Let stand in refrigerator until ready to serve.

Menu No. 9

Entrée

Roast Beef Louis
Roast potatoes
Eggplant Clementina
Cucumbers in sour cream

Dessert

Frosted Mocha cake
Coffee

ROAST BEEF LOUIS

Standing rib roast	*Worcestershire sauce*
(first 3 ribs)	*½ bottle of catsup*
Salt and fresh-ground	*3 onions, sliced*
pepper	*Oven thermometer*
Seasoned salt	

500-DEGREE OVEN (to start)

Remove beef from refrigerator two hours before roasting. Sprinkle with salt, pepper, and seasoned salt. Sprinkle with Worcestershire sauce, then shake catsup over entire roast. Spear slices of onion to the fat with toothpicks. Insert thermometer, be careful that it does not touch bone. Place in preheated 500-degree oven for 25 minutes, then reduce heat to 325 for the remainder of the time. Roast until thermometer registers rare, medium, or well done—whichever you prefer.

Because of the high temperature at the beginning, meat roasts quickly. For rare, it takes about 1 hour and 45 minutes—but trust only your thermometer! Cook enough ahead so that roast can rest on warm platter, beneath aluminum foil, at least half an hour before serving.

ROAST POTATOES

> 12 *medium-sized potatoes*
>   (*old, if possible*)
> 3 *tablespoons butter* (*or*
>   *bacon drippings*)
> *Salt*
> *Paprika*

Peel potatoes and parboil them in boiling salted water to cover, for 5 minutes. Drain well, return to pan, and shake gently over a hot fire for a minute or two to dry. Melt fat in heavy skillet and sauté potatoes until quite brown. Season with salt and paprika, and place in buttered, ovenproof dish. Let stand. When roast beef is removed from the oven, turn heat up to 375 degrees and, just before guests arrive, cover potatoes with aluminum foil and put in oven to bake 30–40 minutes.

BAKED EGGPLANT

No matter how much you make, it won't be enough.

> 2 *tablespoons olive oil*
> 1 *tablespoon butter*
> 4 *large onions, sliced*
> 12 *medium mushrooms,*
>   *sliced*
> 4 *large, peeled tomatoes,*
>   *sliced*
> 3 *small eggplants* (*firm*
>   *and shiny*)
>
> ½ *cup olive oil*
> *Salt and fresh-ground*
>   *pepper*
> *Basil*
> *Parmesan cheese*
> *Herbed bread crumbs*
>   (*come in packages*)
> *Mozzarella cheese*

Heat oil and butter in heavy skillet, add onions, salt them lightly, and sauté over medium heat until soft. Spoon into a bowl. In the same pan sauté the mushrooms (adding a little more butter and oil, if necessary). Spoon into another bowl. Sauté tomatoes in this same pan for a minute or two (again adding more fat, if needed).

Peel and slice eggplants into slices ¼ inch–½ inch thick. Pour ½ cup olive oil on a platter. Lightly dip eggplant slices (on both sides) in the oil, then arrange close together, on a closed cookie tin. Broil in the oven on both sides until slices look lightly toasted.

In the bottom of a large, deep, ungreased casserole, put a layer of eggplant slices. Season with salt and pepper and spoon over some of the onion, then some mushrooms, and a few slices of tomato. Season tomatoes with salt and pepper and a sprinkling of basil and Parmesan cheese. Repeat layers until all ingredients have been used, ending with eggplant on top. Shake bread crumbs over the top and a few thin slices of Mozzarella cheese. Bake for 30 minutes in 375-degree oven in the morning. In the evening finish baking (covered) with the potatoes—same oven temperature, same length of time.

SALAD

> 6 long thin cucumbers
> Finely chopped chives (or parsley)

SOUR-CREAM DRESSING

> 1 cup thick, sour cream   1 teaspoon dry mustard
>   (commercial)   Paprika
> 2 tablespoons vinegar   ½ teaspoon dill weed
> 1 teaspoon salt   1 teaspoon sugar

TO PREPARE THE CUCUMBERS:* Add finely chopped chives.

TO PREPARE DRESSING: Combine all the ingredients in a bowl and mix well. Add cucumbers, fold over until well coated, and pour into a serving dish. Sprinkle chopped chives or parsley across the top and refrigerate until ready to serve.

MOCHA CAKE

6 eggs, separated
1 cup sugar
1 tablespoon Instant
    coffee

1 cup cake flour
1 teaspoon baking powder

350-DEGREE OVEN

FROSTING

1 stick of butter (at room
    temperature)
1 cup confectioners'
    sugar
¼ cup cocoa

Hot strong coffee
    (about ¼ cup)
½ teaspoon vanilla
½ pint heavy cream

TO PREPARE CAKE: In a large bowl (or mixer bowl) beat egg
yolks until thick and lemon-colored. Gradually add sugar and
coffee. Sift together flour and baking powder and add to mixture, all at once. Beat egg whites until stiff and shiny, but not
dry, and fold lightly into mixture. Pour into 2 ungreased 9-
inch cake pans and bake in a 350-degree oven for 12 minutes.
If not brown enough by that time, turn up oven to 400 degrees
for 3–4 minutes longer. When finished, run knife around rim,
cover with an inverted wire cake cooler, turn upside down
and give a tap.

TO PREPARE FROSTING: Cream butter and gradually add sugar
and cocoa. Thin with a little coffee from time to time. Add
vanilla. If the mixture is too thin to spread, add a little more
sugar and cocoa. If too thick, add a little coffee.

Whip cream until stiff, sweeten to taste. Place one layer of
cake on serving plate and frost with whipped cream. Cover
with second layer and spread frosting in swirls across the top
and flatly around the sides. Lightly sprinkle some decoration
on the top—whatever you have available such as parings of
bittersweet or bitter chocolate, ground nuts, etc.

Comment:

Just before guests arrive put potatoes and eggplant in the oven vacated by the roast beef (having raised the temperature to 375 degrees). Put the roast beef on a serving platter and cover with foil. On returning to the kitchen ten minutes before serving, garnish roast beef (sprigs of parsley, watercress, slices of orange—*something!*) and carry food to the table.

Menu No. 10

Entrée

Ragout of beef with mushrooms and onions
Chived, mashed potatoes
Buttered green peas
Sliced tomatoes, vinaigrette

Dessert

Glazed-pear cheese pie
Coffee

RAGOUT OF BEEF

This entire dish not only can, but should, be made the day before. This guarantees delicious, fat-free gravy, and the meat will be better for being reheated.

2–2½ *pounds top round, cut into 2-inch squares*	1 *teaspoon tomato paste*
	3 *tablespoons flour*
	1 *cup beef bouillon*
3 *tablespoons butter*	1 *cup red Burgundy*
2 *tablespoons oil*	*Salt and fresh-ground*
3 *tablespoons hot sherry*	*pepper*
24 *small, white onions, peeled*	*Bouquet of herbs (parsley stems, chives, celery*
16 *medium-sized mushrooms, quartered*	*tops, etc.)*
	Fresh, chopped parsley

Melt butter and oil in a large, heavy skillet and when hot, add as many pieces of beef as possible, without crowding. Brown quickly on all sides, remove to dish to make room for more. (If necessary, add more butter and oil to the pan.) When all the pieces are well browned, return meat to skillet and pour over hot sherry. Stir well, then remove beef with slotted spoon to Dutch oven (or other heavy pan) and put onions in skillet. Turn for a minute, until well coated with pan juices, then add quartered mushrooms and cook for a minute or two longer. Add tomato paste, 1 tablespoon of the flour and stir until blended. Add half the bouillon, mix well, then the second tablespoon flour, balance of bouillon, and last tablespoon flour (mixing and blending with each addition). Bring mixture to a boil, then add ¼ cup Burgundy. Season beef with salt and pepper, and spoon over sauce, mushrooms, and onions. Cook slowly until almost tender (1½–2 hours) adding the remaining wine during this cooking period. Remove beef and mushrooms to the casserole in which it will be served the following day, and arrange onions across the top. Strain gravy into a bowl. Let both cool, then refrigerate until the following late afternoon. Remove from refrigerator an hour before guests are due, and just before they arrive put casserole in a pre-heated 375-degree oven, skim fat from gravy and pour into a small pan. Let stand on stove.

CHIVED, MASHED POTATOES

8 medium-sized, old potatoes
¼ cup hot milk (or cream)

3 tablespoons butter
Salt to taste
2 tablespoons chopped chives

Wash, pare, and quarter potatoes. Cook, in enough boiling, salted water to cover, until *thoroughly* tender. Drain, return to pan and shake, uncovered, over high heat for a minute or two. Remove from stove and crush with potato masher (in the same pan). Beat with large wire whisk (or portable electric beater) until smooth, meanwhile slowly adding the hot milk and butter. Season with salt, add chives, and place the pan in a larger pan of water, *uncovered*. (Or cook potatoes in top of double boiler and place over bottom.) Just before guests arrive, turn on heat. Later, on return to kitchen before serving, stir well so that potatoes will heat through.

BUTTERED GREEN PEAS

2 *packages frozen* tiny
   peas
1 *tablespoon butter*
1 *teaspoon frozen*
   chopped onion

Shake of fresh-ground
   pepper
½ *cup chicken stock*
   (or water)
Salt (if needed—stock
   may be salty)

Just before guests arrive, remove peas from freezer and let stand at room temperature. In the pan in which they will cook, bring butter, onion, stock, and seasoning to a boil. Remove from heat and let stand until ready to use. When you return ten minutes before serving, bring liquid back to a boil and add peas. They will be cooked in 2 minutes. Drain, pour into a serving dish and add a little butter.

SLICED TOMATOES, VINAIGRETTE

6 *medium-to-large ripe, red tomatoes, peeled*
Salt and fresh-ground pepper
Fresh, chopped parsley

VINAIGRETTE SAUCE

1 *teaspoon salt*
⅛ *teaspoon fresh-ground*
   pepper
Shake of cayenne pepper
¼ *teaspoon paprika*
¼ *cup vinegar (your*
   choice)
⅔ *cup salad oil*

1 *teaspoon finely chopped*
   stuffed olives
1 *teaspoon finely chopped*
   capers
1 *teaspoon finely chopped*
   chives
1 *teaspoon finely chopped*
   parsley

Slice tomatoes to any desired thickness and arrange, over-lapping, in the shallow dish in which they will be served. Season lightly with salt and pepper.

TO PREPARE VINAIGRETTE SAUCE (which can be done at your convenience days ahead): Combine the first four items in a small bowl (or mixer bowl). Add vinegar and oil slowly, beating well. Add remaining ingredients and stir lightly until blended. Pour into a bottle with a screw-on top and leave at room temperature until ready to use.

GLAZED-PEAR CHEESE PIE

This, too, can be prepared the day before up to "fruit and glaze." It is one of the very best.

2 eight-ounce packages cream cheese (at room temperature)	⅔ cup sugar ⅛ teaspoon almond extract
3 eggs	

350-DEGREE OVEN

TOPPING

1½ cups sour cream
3 tablespoons sugar
1 teaspoon vanilla

FRUIT AND GLAZE

1 No. 2½ can pear halves (medium size) 1 ten-ounce package frozen strawberries (or raspberries)	½ cup sugar 1½ tablespoons cornstarch

TO PREPARE CHEESE PIE: Put cheese in bowl (or mixer bowl) and beat until light and creamy. Add eggs, *one at a time*, beating thoroughly after each addition. Add sugar and almond extract and continue beating until mixture is smooth, thick, and lemon-colored, (about 5 minutes). Pour into a greased

9-inch pie plate and bake 50 minutes at 350 degrees. Remove from oven (*leaving oven on at same temperature*) and cool for 20 minutes. During that time, *prepare topping* by blending together sour cream, sugar, and vanilla. Spoon topping mixture over top of cheese pie and return to oven for another 15 minutes. When cool, refrigerate. (If making cheese pie on the day it will be served—do not refrigerate.)

TO PREPARE FRUIT AND GLAZE (this is best done only a few hours before serving—cheese pie should be removed from refrigerator by noon together with strawberries, so that they can thaw): Strain thawed fruit into a saucepan. Combine sugar and cornstarch, and after fruit is heated, add mixture and cook until thick and clear, stirring constantly (about 4 minutes). Cool slightly. During that time drain pear halves, pat gently with paper toweling, and arrange on cheese pie, cut side down and stems toward center. If you have an extra pear half —place it in the center. Spoon warm glaze over pears and entire surface of pie. Let stand at room temperature until ready to serve.

Comment:

Just before guests arrive put casserole in preheated 375-degree oven, and skimmed gravy in pan on stove. Bring vegetable liquid to a boil and turn off. Turn on heat under potatoes. On returning to kitchen ten minutes before serving, stir potatoes, turn on heat beneath gravy, bring vegetable liquid back to a boil, add the peas, and cook for about 2–3 minutes. Drain and put in warm serving dish. Add vinaigrette sauce (well shaken) to tomatoes; sprinkle them and casserole with chopped parsley, and bring food to table.

Menu No. 11.

Entrée

Casserole of veal
Fluffy rice
Sautéed broccoli
Mixed green salad

Dessert

Maple mousse
Coffee

CASSEROLE OF VEAL

This casserole can be made the day before and only mushroom caps cooked on the day of the dinner.

2–2½ *pounds lean veal
    cutlets, cut into 1½-
    inch squares*
3 *tablespoons butter*
2 *tablespoons oil*
2 *tablespoons chopped
    frozen onion*
1 *clove of garlic, crushed*
2 *tablespoons flour*
1 *cup chicken stock*

1 *cup dry, white wine*
4 *large, ripe tomatoes,
    peeled, seeded, and
    chopped*
Juice of 1 lemon
*Salt and fresh-ground
    pepper*
18 *medium-to-large
    mushroom caps*
Fresh, chopped parsley
375-DEGREE OVEN (for reheating)

TO PREPARE CASSEROLE: Heat butter and oil in a heavy skillet and sauté veal cubes (avoid crowding pan) until well browned. Remove meat (with a slotted spoon) to Dutch oven (or heavy kettle). In the same pan, sauté chopped onion and crushed garlic clove. Stir in flour, mix well, then add stock, ¼ cup wine, tomatoes, lemon juice, and seasoning. Cook together for a minute or two longer, then pour over veal. Cover Dutch oven tightly and simmer meat for 1½ hours, adding balance of wine from time to time. Pour meat and sauce into serving casserole and cool. (Refrigerate, if made the day before.) Sauté mushrooms in butter for 3–4 minutes, leave in skillet on back of stove. Just before guests arrive, place casserole (having been at room temperature at least 3 hours) in a pre-heated 375-degree oven, covered. Let bake 30–40 minutes.

FLUFFY RICE

1½ *cups unwashed, raw rice*	*3 tablespoons salt*
	3 tablespoons butter
Large pan containing 6–7 quarts rapidly boiling water	*¼ teaspoon salt*
	White pepper
	Buttered, wax paper
	350-DEGREE OVEN

Boil rice, uncovered, until barely tender. Pour into a colander and hold under running *hot* water for a minute. While rice is cooking, melt butter, with seasonings, in the casserole in which rice will be served. Have casserole standing in a pan of boiling water. Pour drained rice into hot casserole and fluff with 2 forks so that butter and seasonings blend with the rice. Cover casserole with buttered wax paper, then the casserole cover, and place (still in the pan of hot water) in the lower portion of 350-degree oven. Bake for 30 minutes. Fluff again, cover, and set aside to be reheated in the casserole, over a pan of simmering water, during cocktails.

BROCCOLI

2 *bunches broccoli*	*2 tablespoons butter*
Salt and fresh-ground pepper	*1 tablespoon oil*

Soak broccoli in cold water for 10–15 minutes. Drain. Remove large leaves and tough ends of stalk. Make deep gashes in the bottom of stalks and place in a saucepan containing 1½ inch of boiling, salted water. Cover tightly and cook over medium heat for 10 minutes. Drain and season. Heat butter and oil in heavy skillet and gently sauté broccoli for about 5 minutes. Arrange in an ovenproof serving dish and let cool. When casserole of veal comes out of oven, turn up broiler and broil broccoli until sizzling hot.

MIXED GREEN SALAD

Salad greens (Bibb lettuce, romaine, endive, celery tops, etc.)

French dressing*

Fresh, chopped herbs (dill, tarragon, chives— whatever available)

8 radishes, sliced thin

Fresh, chopped parsley

Wash and dry salad greens. Place on paper-towel-lined salad bowl and refrigerate. Slice radishes and chop herbs—place in separate pieces of wax paper and store on top of salad greens. Prepare French dressing and let stand at room temperature. Just before serving, lightly salt salad greens, add herbs, then French dressing, and toss until well coated. Scatter radish slices over top of bowl, sprinkle with parsley, and a twist of pepper.

MAPLE MOUSSE

¾ cup maple syrup

3 egg yolks (well-beaten)

3 egg whites (stiffly beaten)

Few grains of salt

1½ cups heavy cream, whipped

1 teaspoon vanilla

Heat syrup in the top of double boiler. Slowly add the egg yolks and beat over simmering water until thick and light. Pour mixture over beaten egg whites, add salt, and chill thoroughly in refrigerator. When cold, add whipped cream and vanilla. Pour into refrigerator trays (or lightly oiled mold). Freeze, without stirring, for several hours.

Comment:

Just before guests arrive put casserole in preheated 375-degree oven and place rice casserole over gently simmering water. On returning to the kitchen, remove casserole, turn oven up to broil, and place broccoli beneath fire until sizzling hot. Meanwhile toss salad and fluff rice. Carry everything to the table.

Menu No. 12

Entrée

Baked steak, piquante
Potato halves, baked
Braised celery
Whole stuffed tomatoes

Dessert

Orange cake
Coffee

BAKED STEAK, PIQUANTE

Sirloin steak, 3 inches
*   thick*
Salt and fresh-ground
*   pepper*
1 medium-sized onion,
*   grated*
1 cup catsup

3 tablespoons butter,
*   melted*
1 tablespoon lemon juice
1 small green pepper,
*   sliced*
Fresh, chopped parsley

425-DEGREE OVEN

MUSTARD SAUCE

2 tablespoons butter
2 tablespoons prepared
*   barbecue sauce*

2 teaspoons
*   Worcestershire sauce*
2 teaspoons dry mustard
2 tablespoons cream

TO PREPARE STEAK: Preheat broiler until very hot, place steak in a pan 4 inches below broiler and quickly sear both sides. Remove pan, drain off fat, season with salt and pepper, and add onion, catsup, Worcestershire sauce, butter, lemon juice, and green pepper. Just before guests arrive, place in 400-degree oven to bake for 45 minutes.

TO PREPARE THE SAUCE: Melt butter in a small pan and add barbecue sauce, Worcestershire sauce, and dry mustard, blending together with a small wire whisk. Put aside until ten minutes before serving—then heat sauce, add cream, and cook over medium heat just long enough to heat cream. Pour over steak, and sprinkle lavishly with fresh, chopped parsley.

POTATO HALVES, BAKED

4–5 large baking potatoes
Vegetable shortening
Salt

Wash and dry potatoes. Cut in half (lengthwise) and score tops in ½" squares, making cuts about ½" deep. Brush tops and skins with vegetable shortening, place in pan and bake with steak—same temperature, same length of time. (Should be golden brown when finished.)

BRAISED CELERY

6 celery hearts
4 ounces butter
*1 tablespoon chopped
    frozen onion*
*Salt and fresh-ground
    pepper*

*1½ cups beef consommé
    (or stock)*
*½ teaspoon beef extract
    (or glace de viande,
    or beef bouillon
    cube)*

Trim off outer stalks and leaves of celery and cut in half, lengthwise. Melt one half of the butter in a pan, add onion, and sauté for a few minutes for medium heat. Arrange celery on top, season, and add one half of the consommé. Cover the pan and simmer for 20 minutes. Blend beef extract with the liquid in the pan, add the balance of the butter and consommé, and put aside, uncovered, until evening. Bake, uncovered, in same oven, same length of time, as the steak and potatoes.

STUFFED TOMATOES

6 *medium-to-large ripe*
  tomatoes
Salt and fresh-ground
  pepper

Powdered dill (or finely
  chopped fresh)
6 *canned artichoke hearts*
Fresh, chopped parsley

SAUCE

1 *cup mayonnaise*
½ *cup sour cream*

1 *teaspoon lemon juice*
1 *teaspoon grated onion*

Skin tomatoes and cut off a top slice—enough to enable you to scoop out insides. Turn upside down on a paper-towel-lined platter to drain for a few minutes. Season inside and out with salt and pepper and a little dill. Place an artichoke inside each, and refrigerate. Combine ingredients for sauce, pour into a bowl, and refrigerate. On returning to the kitchen before serving, arrange tomatoes on serving platter and pour over mayonnaise dressing. Sprinkle with fresh, chopped parsley.

ORANGE CAKE

6 *egg yolks*
4 *egg whites* ⎱ in separate bowls
2 *egg whites* ⎰
3 *teaspoons water*
1 *cup sugar, sifted*
1 *cup all-purpose flour,*
  sifted

1 *teaspoon baking powder*
Grated peel of 1 orange
Grated peel of 1 lemon

350-DEGREE OVEN

TOPPING

2 *egg whites* (from
   above)
¾ *cup orange juice*
Juice of 1 small lemon
¾ *cup sugar*

½ *pint whipping cream*
1 *small can mandarin*
   oranges
Grated orange peel

Place egg yolks in large bowl (or large mixer bowl), add water, and beat until well blended. Add sugar gradually, beating until mixture is thick and lemon-colored. Sift together sifted flour and baking powder and fold into mixture. Add orange and lemon peel. Beat 4 egg whites until they stand in peaks and fold lightly (with a metal spoon) into batter. Pour into ungreased, 9-inch springform and bake for 50 minutes in a 350-degree oven. Turn off heat but let cake remain in *unopened* oven until the oven is cold.

TO PREPARE THE TOPPING: Beat the 2 egg whites until foamy but not stiff, then beat in orange juice, lemon juice, and sugar. With a heavy match (or skewer) poke holes all over top of cake and slowly pour the liquid over the holes. Let stand for 1 hour. Whip cream, sweeten to taste, and frost cake with the whipped cream. Drain mandarin oranges and decorate outer top edge and sides with them. Grate orange peel over the top for added color. Keep in a cool place (or the bottom of the refrigerator) until ready to serve.

Comment:

Just before guests arrive, steak, potatoes, and celery go into 425-degree oven. Ten minutes before serving, baste steak, arrange tomatoes and cover with mayonnaise and chopped parsley, and heat sauce for steak. Remove steak to hot platter, pour over sauce and add parsley, and surround with baked potato halves.

PART TWO

Kitchen Maneuvers

5

Make Your Food Lovely to Look At

The food on the platter may be the most delicious ever prepared by gifted hands, but if it doesn't look attractive, half the magic is missing. Conversely, the most ordinary edibles will take on allure if presented with imagination. A platter of sliced ham, Swiss cheese, and rye bread is useful on occasion, even though routine and unimaginative fare. But when alternate rows of tightly rolled ham and thinly sliced cheese are separated by dill pickles and tomato wedges; when sprigs of parsley bedeck the platter; when, close by, stand baskets of buttered, crustless rye bread and two kinds of mustard—watch out, you may get hurt in the crush.

Arriving at the Cordon Bleu one foggy London day at the beginning of my course, I gazed with distaste at the various ingredients spread out on the long, wooden table in the center of the room. Where were the makings of those elegant French dishes in this hodgepodge of pedestrian ingredients? Flour, sugar, eggs, a bit of chocolate, rice, a small chicken, green peppers, a little parsley, a tomato or two, and other odds and ends. Conspicuously unattractive was a very dead haddock (though bright of eye) that looked hopelessly unappetizing.

Obviously peasant stuff—can this be gourmet cooking, I wondered.

Two hours later I had my answer. By that time the freshly scrubbed table had been transformed into a bewitching buffet on which, artfully displayed with eye for photogenic splendor, reposed such items as a shining copper tureen filled with fragrant, spicy tomato soup; a small, crisply browned baked chicken, redolent of fresh herbs; and a beguiling chocolate cake, whose smooth, light frosting fairly danced with tight little curlicues of chocolate.

But the indisputable, show-stealing star of the day was the fish. Skinned, boned, and cut into thick chunks, it had been rolled in seasoned flour and quickly fried in oil. Now, resting on a bed of fluffy rice, it lay flanked on one side by bright-green, sliced, cooked peppers, on the other by lightly fried tomato slices, while over the top had been spooned a delicate curry sauce with a covering of onion rings. A sprinkling of bright-green parsley over all, a gravy boat filled with the balance of the sauce, and a bowl of chutney completed this savory picture. Peasant fare indeed!

It was at the Cordon Bleu that I first discovered that almost any dish can be made ahead. Including fish. This very dish that I have just described was taken home by me and served the following evening. The sprinkling of parsley was omitted until just before serving, and I was instructed to cover the dish with "buttered, greaseproof paper" (the English equivalent of aluminum foil) and place in a 400-degree oven for about 15 minutes, after which I should remove the paper and "run the dish" under a hot broiler for another 3–4 minutes. It tasted every bit as good as it looked. As you have seen, it is possible to cook most food ahead, with the exception of fresh peas (that shrivel), hot soufflés (that collapse), and sundry other items.

While parsley is by no means the only garnish of charm, it works wonders for the dishes it adorns. I do not mean the sprigs of parsley that decorate a platter. For this a bouquet of mint, water cress, or, failing all else, lilac leaves will do as well. I refer to fresh, bright-green, finely chopped, confetti-like **parsley** that can be sprinkled over salads, omelets, roasts, potatoes, soups, and vegetables to the benefit of all concerned. If you don't believe in the potency of its charm, try exposing your guests to a buffet on which stand individual salads, half of which have had the parsley treatment. These will vanish before the others are touched, as I demonstrated to my disbelieving husband not long ago. Once you have become enamored of confettilike parsley, food served without it looks stark naked. *Here's How:*

Put enough ordinary, **unwashed** parsley to fill your needs for two or three days on your wooden chopping board and cut off the stems. (Store these stems in the salad drawer of your refrigerator and add them to soups, casseroles, the insides of chickens, etc., as most of the parsley flavor is in the stems.) Using your heaviest, sharpest knife, hold the tip down firmly on the chopping board with your left hand (as lever) and chop the parsley rapidly back and forth (in small semicircles) with your right hand until it is finely chopped. By this time it will look limp, damp, and unattractive. Spoon this mess into a clean, heavy dishcloth (that has been rinsed under cold water and tightly wrung out). Fold the corners to form a tight bag and hold it under running, cold water, rinsing and squeezing out the water a few times. This cleans the parsley right through the bag and starts the magic. One last hard squeeze to eliminate every drop of water possible, then back to the wooden board. Spread out a double thickness of paper towel, open the bag and turn out contents on the paper toweling. Your dank, soggy mess is now a thing of light-green, fluffy beauty. Store half the parsley on paper toweling in a small, wide-mouthed, *open* jar at the back of your workspace and bank the rest, folded in paper toweling, inside your refrigerator. If not used within about three days, the worst that can happen is that you will have some colorful, dried parsley on hand.

If you happen to have a garden, ten cents' worth of parsley seed, planted in the early spring, will keep you handsomely supplied for most of the year. Although slow to germinate, it lasts until the first frost, survives the winter, and can be used for a month or two the following spring before growing large and tough. By that time the new crop will be sprouting.

Mint, given half a chance, will take over your garden and be perennially on hand from early spring until frost, year in, year out. Once planted, it requires nothing further than a bit of shade each day and, from time to time, some ruthless thinning. It makes a stunning garnish for meat or dessert platters, attractively adorns iced drinks, and is beautiful in flower arrangements. Water cress is another charmer but hard to come by.

To Make Food Look More Alluring

Surround mounded chicken salad with small, seedless **grapes,** dot the top with **capers,** and sprinkle with chopped **dill.**

Cover pot roast, broilers, stuffed veal chops, hamburgers, etc., with whole, broiled **mushroom caps.**

Scatter tiny **gherkin pickles,** sliced and fanned, over cold meat or sandwich platters.

Glamorize vegetables such as asparagus, broccoli, beans, etc., with **slivered almonds,** toasted brown in a little butter. (These, too, will stand and wait.)

Decorate the salad platter with **tomato slices,** dipped in chopped parsley or chives. Or, when in season, scatter cherry or yellow plum tomatoes across the top of the bowl.

Rice **cream cheese** lightly over salad greens after they have been tossed in a tart French dressing. Then sprinkle with chopped chives.

Add **young spinach** leaves to the greens in the salad bowl.

Sprinkle **grated cheese** over clear, hot soup, spaghetti, any creamed dish, and salads—choice of cheese depending on dish in hand.

Add slivers of **green peppers** to the salad bowl or decorate fish or meat platters with mounds of Julienne strips of pepper.

Crumble crisp **bacon** over the salad bowl after the greens are tossed. This also makes a nice contrast in texture when sprinkled over mashed or baked, stuffed potatoes.

Cut green, leafy **celery tops** into the salad bowl for added color (and flavor).

Stab thick **lemon wedges** with plastic spears (from the five-and-ten) and serve them with fish, tomato juice, Bloody Marys, lobster salad, etc.—any dish that might be improved by the addition of extra lemon juice to taste.

Ring the salad platter with **cherry tomatoes,** cut in two and stuffed with cottage cheese mixed with seasonings and chives.

As you may have gathered—it is my feeling that a whipped-cream surface without garnish looks as bleakly bare as a dinner table without a centerpiece. Depending on under-pinnings—grate **nuts, chocolate, lemon rind, orange rind,** etc., over top.

Pile ice cream in a mold, combining several flavors, and dribble chocolate or butterscotch sauce over every few scoops. When unmolded, it makes an attractive pattern, and tastes good besides.

To make **chocolate curlicues**—scrape squares of semisweet or bitter chocolate with a vegetable parer, using big and little strokes, to make a variety of shavings.

To retain the bright, **green** color of vegetables (such as asparagus, string beans, broccoli, etc.), rinse quickly and gently under running cold water immediately after removing from the stove. This is called "refreshing" the vegetable and is an especially useful device when putting aside to reheat, later, under foil and butter sauce.

Alternating tiny bunches of parsley, lemon wedges, and sliced, hard-cooked eggs, gives added appeal to the fish platter.

One word of warning: "Lovely to look at" is no substitute for delicious, interesting food and you can't fool anyone with handsome garnishes or feathery parsley for more than a minute or two. But combined with well-seasoned, delectable food, they can boost you to stardom.

6

Make it Taste Better

How paradoxical that we, who so fearlessly change the styles of our dresses, hats, shoes, or hairdos, are so timid when it comes to new styles in cooking.

Take the matter of herbs. For some reason most of us start out by being afraid of them (as we are of omelets, soufflés, meringues, Hollandaise sauce, and other concoctions that, on closer acquaintance, prove to be no more scary than pillbox hats). Herbs add flavor, color, fragrance, and sophistication to the dishes they glorify. Since many excellent charts and books are available on this subject, I shall limit myself to a few suggestions.

The ideal way to overcome fear in the use of herbs is to grow them in your garden, if you happen to have one. A small, simple herb garden is such a miracle of fragrant beauty, with its contrasting greens and delicate flowers, that it seems only natural to snip those alluringly pungent greens for the salad bowl, omelet, or casserole, and thus away you go. Such a garden takes up very little room and those lovely greens are packed with vitamins.

For a starter, I suggest such perennials as chives, garlic

chives, tarragon, thyme, lovage, and burnet (including, of course, those indispensable loves of my life—parsley and mint); such annuals as chervil, basil, and dill. (One small package of dill will reseed itself all over the garden, but there is no such thing as too much fresh dill.)

If you have no garden, a few fresh herbs can be purchased in small pots (notably chives and parsley), and almost all of them come in jars of dried herbs. These are very good—just make certain that they are a bright-green color when you purchase them (the brighter, the better). Brown, overaged herbs taste like straw, so check your shelves from time to time and bravely toss out those that are no longer green. Dried herbs are approximately three times stronger than fresh, hence must be used in that proportion except for such mild ones as parsley, chervil, or dill.

"Bouquet garni" means a few sprigs of different herbs tied together and added to the pot during the last half hour of cooking (and well worth the bother). Such a bouquet might consist of 6 parsley stems, 2 sprigs of thyme, a small bunch of lovage leaves (or celery tops), and ½ bay leaf. If using dried herbs, tie them together in a piece of cheesecloth. Fresh or dried, they provide wonderful flavoring for soups, pot roasts, stews, casseroles, etc. Tie a string around the middle of your *bouquet garni* and leave the end hanging out over the edge of the pot, thus making it easy to fish out.

"Fines herbes" are a combination of herbs, fresh chopped or dried, that become part of the dish it flavors. A good combination might be chives, chervil, tarragon, and parsley. Your recipe will suggest what proportions to use—but when you have had experience, you will enjoy choosing your own. These are used most often in egg or cheese dishes, sprinkled over the salad bowl, or with fish, roasts, and soup.

If you are a stranger to herbs, a book on the subject will teach you the foods for which each has a special affinity (such as basil for tomatoes, mint for lamb, chervil for eggs, tarragon for chicken, dill for boiled potatoes, etc.). You will also learn the combinations that complement each other (such as basil, thyme, and burnet; or tarragon, chervil, and parsley). In your garden you will discover that lovage tastes like celery, burnet like cucumbers, and that garlic-chives are a delicate compound of their double name. Only by experimenting, not only with herbs but spices and other flavorings, can you discover which ones you and/or your guests prefer. At one time or another recipes will call for cloves, curry, ginger, poppy seeds, saffron, soy sauce, capers, anchovies, caraway seeds, and dozens of other ingredients. If you are dubious about any one of them, omit or try a substitute. Experimenting is the way new and improved recipes are discovered.

Now is as good a time as any to sing the praises of four valiant flavors, without which food would be considerably diminished for me. In the order of their importance they are lemon, onion, garlic, and celery. Fresh lemon juice (there is no substitute) brings out the flavor and improves anything it touches; onion invites and excites; garlic (discreetly used) makes food scale epicurean heights; and celery supplies a welcome freshness and texture to the food it accompanies.

Random Herb Recommendations

THE SALAD BOWL

Add some or all of the following, depending on your mood and tastes: chopped lovage, burnet, chives, chervil, parsley, tarragon, and dill. These are all mild. With the exception of parsley, "chopped herbs" means finely cut with kitchen shears. If using dried herbs, blend them for a few minutes in the dressing (thus releasing the flavor), before tossing the salad.

FRESH PEAS

Add finely chopped mint, just before serving.

COTTAGE CHEESE

Add chopped chives, parsley, tarragon, salt, fresh-ground pepper, celery salt, and 1 tablespoon sour cream, per half pint. Before serving, dust with paprika.

TOMATO JUICE

Several hours before serving, to each quart of juice add 1 teaspoon each of chopped chives, basil, and parsley, 2 tablespoons lemon juice, and 1 teaspoon celery salt.

OMELET OR SCRAMBLED EGGS

Add a mixture of finely chopped parsley, tarragon, dill, and chives, to the *melted butter in the pan before adding the eggs.* This will bring out the flavor of the herbs and make the eggs look irresistible.

HAMBURGERS

Mix the meat with salt, fresh-ground pepper, and a generous mixture of finely chopped chives, tarragon, and parsley. Let stand at room temperature for at least half an hour before cooking. See Hamburger *Diane,** if you want to transform it into company fare.

HERB BUTTER

A jar of herb butter stored in the refrigerator, can give an exquisite touch to vegetables, meat, fish, and sandwiches (or appetizers). Use 2 ounces unsalted butter with 1 tablespoon chopped green herbs or 1 teaspoon dried. The butter should be creamed first and a few drops of lemon juice added. You will find it hard to go wrong, no matter which herbs you choose. Top broiled food with the butter just before serving as the butter would scorch beneath the fire. A wonderful improvement to fish.

From herbs to wine is a natural step, for wine supplies flavor, aroma, and a special deliciousness to the food it enhances. Subtly used, it can elevate the commonplace to Olympian heights. But let anyone take one bite of your food and murmur, "ah, wine," and you can chalk up a failure. Wine is intended to charm and mystify, not assault the palate.

Flavor, not alcoholic content, provides the lift from wine, when added to cooking food. Since the alcohol is both superfluous and harsh, it is a good idea to get rid of it. Here is another simple procedure that scares even experienced cooks. To "blaze" wine (burn off the alcohol), pour the required amount into a saucepan over medium heat. Just before it comes to a boil, quickly hold a lighted match over the pan. The liquid will ignite at once and continue burning (even when the liquid boils hard) until the alcohol is gone. It is now ready for use. For some dishes the liquid is "blazed" after being poured over the food (such as cognac flaming over crepes suzette, or chafing-dish lobster ablaze with rum).

Suggestions for Cooking With Wine or Liqueurs

Most hot soups are improved by the addition of a tablespoon or two of **sherry** or **Madeira** to each bowl.

A **cup of red wine,** added gradually to the liquid in which a pot roast or stew is simmering, adds flavor and strength to the gravy and tenderness to the meat.

Add any drops of **leftover wine** to gravies, casseroles, or vinegars.

A **marinade** composed of one part vinegar, one part Worcestershire sauce, five parts Burgundy, and ten parts oil will tenderize and improve the flavor of steak or chops. Have meat at room temperature and brush on marinade about four hours before broiling. Turn occasionally. When time to cook, put meat under flame, marinade and all.

Dry, white wine enhances the delicate flavor of chicken or fish. On the other hand, chicken cooked in red wine is the classic *coq au vin,* and mighty good, too.

Sherry or **vermouth** complement and improve the flavor of lobster stew.

Powdered sugar and either **kirsch, sherry,** or **rum,** sprinkled over fresh pineapple not only give it a delectable flavor, but the longer the fruit stands, the better it becomes.

A bowl of fresh strawberries, lightly sugared and marinated in **champagne,** give that elegant fruit new flavor and glamour.

A tablespoon of **crème de cacao** poured over each scoop of French vanilla ice cream is an excellent substitute for sweet sauces.

Whipped cream is improved by the addition of almost any **liqueur** that you happen to have in hand.

Crème de menthe adds new interest to chocolate sauce, lemon sherbet, or a fruit cup.

To Make Food Taste Better, Add:

Caviar and a few drops of grated onion to mayonnaise, when making chicken or lamb sandwiches.

Thin slices of **lemon** to seasoned lamb as it goes into the oven.

Ginger-garlic powder (comes already blended) to roast chicken or lamb.

Herb mustard to first one side, then the other, of broiling hamburgers.

Chopped mint to honey. Let stand a few hours in the refrigerator—then strain over melon balls.

Grated, sharp Cheddar to fresh-baked, still-warm, apple pie.

Garlic powder and a sprinkling of **dried marjoram** to the butter melting in the pan just before sautéeing mushrooms.

Light-brown sugar to a bowl of washed, stemmed, seedless grapes. Let stand a few hours in the refrigerator—serve cold with sour cream.

Curry powder to mayonnaise when making chicken or lobster salad.

Miscellaneous Suggestions

Raw egg yolks, beaten with a little cream, will thicken soup, sauces, or gravies, far more delicately than flour.

Wherever possible, substitute **stock** (the broth in which meat, poultry, or vegetables was cooked) in place of water. For example, noodles cooked in chicken broth (especially if they are not having any special treatment) are much tastier than when cooked in water.

Tomatoes! Whether serving them whole, sliced, or cut into fat wedges—fresh, garden tomatoes are much more attractive peeled. Put a few at a time in a large bowl, cover with boiling water, let stand for a minute and take out. Slit the skin with a sharp paring knife and the peel will come off in large strips.

On the other hand, when tomatoes are scarce, or the salad bowl requires only the addition of a little color, **"concassed"** tomatoes make a fine decoration. To "concass" tomatoes—cut into quarters, unpeeled, and remove the insides (these can be added to soup or stews), leaving only the red shells. Cut these into narrow strips. Lightly marinated in French dressing and scattered over the salad bowl, slaw, cucumbers, etc., they add both interest and flavor. One lone tomato, *concassed*, can make a big difference, and sometimes that is all you have on hand.

Make an adventure of cooking—what appeals to you will probably please your guests, too. But no matter how reliable the recipe, nor how faithfully you have followed it, taste, taste, TASTE. Maybe it's perfect, but maybe it isn't. Perhaps the addition of a little of this or a shake of that will make the difference between flatness or well-seasoned food. In any case, find out.

No matter how splendid the acting, if an actress muffs her lines, she can spoil the performance. By the same token, no matter how superb the cooking, if a hostess-cook serves hot food on cold plates, she can spoil the dinner. Stars are never guilty of either.

7

Tips and Short Cuts

"It's much harder if you don't know how," has been a slogan in our family ever since an inexperienced cook tried to induce my mother to hire her at top wages, on the strength of this peculiar reasoning.

Only last spring a visiting friend asked if she could help me in the kitchen and was promptly handed a simmering pan of hard-cooked eggs to shell. When I caught up with her some time later, frustrated though determined, she was laboriously picking fragments of shell from considerably mutilated eggs. Hence:

Extras About Eggs

After removing hard-cooked eggs from the stove, place them, still in the pan, under running, cold water for 3–4 minutes. Let stand in cold water a little longer, then briskly spank eggs on sides and ends with a flat, heavy knife. This takes one second per egg, shatters the membrane, and even the freshest of eggs (always the hardest to peel) will slip gracefully out of its shell.

To divide one whole raw egg in two (when halving a recipe that calls for only one), beat the egg in a measuring glass. It will then be easy to divide.

For whiter, easier-cutting **meringue**—add a few drops of lemon juice to the whites before beating.

Add an extra egg white (or two) to a **soufflé** to boost it higher.

Use a **leftover egg yolk** by dropping gently into boiling water and letting simmer until hard cooked. Grated over the salad bowl, or green vegetables, it makes a handsome garnish. Nice on appetizers, too.

To keep leftover egg yolks a few days in the refrigerator, cover with cold water. When ready to use, gently pour off water. Yolks will be intact.

When **separating** yolks from whites, a speck of yolk, accidentally dropped into the whites, will adhere to a piece of bread and can easily be retrieved.

For best results, have eggs at **room temperature** before using —whether scrambling them for breakfast or beating for a meringue.

Freezer Facts

Everyone does not have, nor need, a freezer. City dwellers get along fine without freezers packed with ready-to-serve casseroles, baked desserts, favorite bread, varieties of ice cream, etc. But city dweller or no—if you have a modern refrigerator, you possess freezer space that can be invaluable.

Take the matter of **coffee cream.** We happen to drink ours black, but naturally buy cream when we entertain. Inevitably half a jar stands in the refrigerator until it turns sour. Or did, until I discovered this trick. Instead of buying coffee cream, I now buy whipping cream for guests (to date no one has complained). Whatever is leftover gets whipped, and frozen immediately in a small jar. Thus I have a garnish for desserts such as chocolate mousse, always on hand. To use as whipped cream—*defrost in the refrigerator*. To use again as coffee cream—*defrost at room temperature*.

Chives, as you may have gathered, are an important item in our cuisine. They can be purchased frozen, but to date are not easy to find. Even if you grow them in your garden, keep a supply in the freezer against bad weather, cold weather, or winter. *To freeze*—cut long blades, wash, dry, and remove brown or imperfect ones. Cut very fine and store in a small container in freezer space. When needed, scrape with a fork right into whatever dish you are preparing. They defrost at once and remain bright green and full-flavored. You can also do this with a pot of chives that you buy and which is guaranteed to dry out quickly in your kitchen.

Both egg whites and yolks freeze extremely well. The former require no special treatment; the latter must be lightly beaten with 1 teaspoon salt per cup of beaten yolks. I have learned the hard way that both need to have the exact number written clearly on the container.

Leftover gravy, stock, sauce, white meat of chicken, sandwiches, etc. can be frozen in a small space and kept conveniently on tap when needed.

Miscellaneous Maneuvers

When **quartering lemons** (or dividing them into six or eight wedges apiece)—slice them, then, with a sharp knife, cut off the white pith along the cut edge. This not only improves their appearance, but prevents the juice from squirting.

To **chop dates**—cut them into small pieces with kitchen shears dipped lightly, from time to time, in flour to prevent sticking.

Lightly buttering **leftover sandwiches** on the following day and then toasting them, makes them as good as new. Cut into quarters, they become quick hors d'oeuvres for unexpected company.

When **frying bacon**—do not separate the slices before placing them in the pan as they slide apart easily, when warm, and are apt to tear when cold. When frying bacon for several people—do so ahead, even by an hour or two. Deposit the cooked, crisp bacon on paper toweling on a small, closed, cookie tin. Cover with more toweling (layer, if making a large quantity) and keep warm in a 200-degree oven. The bacon will taste every bit as good as though fresh made, and this procedure will save a lot of time as family and friends drift in for breakfast at different times.

This can also be done with **pancakes**. Make them ahead and place them, overlapping, on a shallow, ovenproof dish (or pan). Brush them with melted buter and store in the same 200-degree oven. As each member of the household appears for breakfast, put his portion on a pie tin and run under a hot broiler. In one minute they will be sizzling and uniquely delicious.

8

Recipes, Recipes, Recipes

As a rock collects barnacles, so do we, who love cooking, accumulate recipes. In time a favored few become symbols of our hospitality and are nostalgically requested by visiting family and friends. Here are some of ours. The quantities given are intended for six, but every hostess-cook knows only too well the variables of starving versus calorie-conscious guests, and will be guided accordingly.

Soups

SPICY TOMATO SOUP

This soup is a great favorite at the Cordon Bleu restaurant in London where it achieved overnight fame, thanks to the coronation of Queen Elizabeth. When The Cordon Bleu School of Cookery was engaged to cater the coronation lunch for four hundred guests, its proposed menu included this soup. Buckingham Palace authorities balked. The luncheon was to be held away from the palace; cooking space was limited, guests many, and soup superfluous in June. Not at all, countered the Cordon Bleu. Guests would be hungry and tired by one o'clock, many would have traveled to London from outlying districts, and what is more reviving than good, hot soup. Buckingham Palace went down in defeat and the Cordon Bleu made history. June 2, 1953, was cold and rainy, and the soup was the hit of the Queen's luncheon. It has been the hit of a good many of ours, too.

2 tablespoons butter
2 onions, sliced thin
2 tablespoons flour
1 teaspoon paprika
5 cups chicken consommé
2 pounds tomatoes (fresh or canned)
Bouquet garni (*parsley stems, celery tops, chives, dill—whatever you have—tied together*)
Peel of 1 lemon
5 whole cloves
1 teaspoon tomato paste
1 cup Burgundy
Salt and fresh-ground pepper
1 tablespoon arrowroot }
2 tablespoons cold water } mixed together
Fresh, chopped parsley

Melt the butter in a deep pan and sauté onion very slowly until soft. Remove from stove and stir in flour and paprika. Return to stove, bring to a boil, and cook for a minute or two. Add consommé, tomatoes (quartered and coarsely chopped, if fresh), herbs, lemon peel, cloves, and tomato paste. Simmer, covered, over low heat for 45 minutes. Strain, and return to stove. In a small, separate pan, warm the Burgundy, ignite, and burn off alcohol. Add to the soup. Season with salt and pepper, tasting carefully as both consommé and wine will give a salty taste. Bring soup to a boil and add arrowroot mixture to thicken slightly. Simmer for a few minutes more. (Can be made days ahead and freezes very well. Omit wine until time of reheating if preparing ahead.) Serve in hot bowls and sprinkle with parsley.

POTAGE PAUL

2 tablespoons butter
2 tablespoons vegetable
  oil
4 tablespoons frozen
  chopped onion
1 clove of garlic
2 tablespoons curry
  powder
2 cups shelled peas
  (or 1 box frozen)

½ cup water
Salt and fresh-ground
  pepper
4 tablespoons flour
6 cups chicken consommé
1 cup light cream
1 pound shredded white
  meat of cooked
  chicken

Heat together butter and oil in a saucepan, add onion and
garlic, and cook slowly for 3–4 minutes. Add curry powder,
mix well, and cook slowly for another 5 minutes. Add peas,
water, salt and pepper, and cook slowly until peas are tender.
Remove from fire, add flour, blend well, return to heat and
slowly add consommé, stirring constantly until soup boils. Pour
through a fine strainer into another saucepan, add the cream
and shredded chicken. Adjust the seasoning to taste, reheat
and serve.

MUSHROOM SOUP

This is a fine way to dispose of stems if the caps have
achieved a more glamorous fate.

4 tablespoons butter
2 tablespoons frozen,
  chopped onion
½ pound mushrooms
  (or stems from 1
  pound)

Salt and fresh-ground
  pepper
2 tablespoons fresh lemon
  juice
½ cup light cream
½ cup sherry
Chopped, fresh parsley

Melt the butter in the top of a double boiler (using it over
direct heat). Add onion, let cook until soft, meanwhile chopping the mushrooms very fine. Add mushrooms to pan and

cook slowly for 10 minutes, stirring occasionally. Remove from stove, add flour, blend well, return pan to heat and boil for a minute or two. Add consommé slowly, and bring to a boil. Season to taste with salt and pepper, add lemon juice, and place pan over bottom of double boiler (filled with simmering water). Cook 30 minutes, add cream and wine, adjust seasoning, and cook until hot. Do not strain—ladle into soup bowls and garnish with parsley.

CLEMENTINA'S TURKEY SOUP

1 turkey carcass (bones, skin, and bits of leftover meat)
8–10 cups of water (depending on size of turkey)
¼ cup chopped carrots
¼ cup chopped celery (including leaves)
¼ cup chopped frozen onions

Parsley stems
1 tablespoon fresh-chopped dill (or ½ tablespoon dried)
4 chicken cubes
Salt and fresh-ground pepper
Any leftover gravy
Any leftover dressing
¼–½ cup white wine (dry)

Cut turkey into small pieces, place in large pan, add water, and bring to a boil. Simmer, covered, for 1½ hours. Add vegetables, herbs, chicken cubes, and seasoning, and simmer for another 1½ hours. Cool, remove bones and skin, strain the soup, extract any small pieces of meat with a fork, put vegetables through a course strainer (or food mill), and return bits of meat and vegetables to the soup and return to stove. Add leftover gravy and dressing (as well as any previously cooked vegetables that might be in the refrigerator) and reheat. Add wine just before serving.

ONION SOUP

6 cups thinly sliced
    yellow onions (about
    2 pounds)
6 tablespoons butter
2 tablespoons vegetable oil
1 teaspoon salt
¼ teaspoon sugar
½ teaspoon dry mustard
3 tablespoons flour

8 cups hot beef bouillon
    (or stock, consommé,
    etc.)
1 cup dry white wine
    (Chablis is excellent)
Salt and fresh-ground
    pepper to taste
Grated Parmesan cheese
6 toasted bread rounds

Heat butter and oil in a 4-quart saucepan (with cover), add onions, cover, and cook slowly for 20 minutes. Uncover pan, add salt, sugar, and mustard, and cook over medium heat until onions are a deep, dark brown (about 40 minutes). Remove from heat, add flour, and blend well. Return to fire, bring to a boil, and add bouillon, then wine. Simmer, partially covered, for 30 minutes more. Adjust seasoning and pour into individual soup bowls. Sprinkle with Parmesan cheese, add toast rounds, and serve.

SUNDAY-NIGHT SOUP (quick and good)

2 cans condensed tomato
    soup
2 cans condensed pea
    soup

2 twelve-ounce bottles
    of beer
2 cups of milk
2 cans (6½-ounces each)
    king crabmeat

Heat together soups, beer, and milk, but keep just below boiling point. When hot, add crabmeat, heat through, and serve with toasted garlic loaf.*

LOBSTER BISQUE (also quick and good)

2 *cans condensed asparagus soup*	2 *cups lobster meat (fresh or canned) shredded*
2 *cans condensed mushroom soup*	½ *cup sherry*
2 *cups light cream*	3 *tablespoons finely chopped chives*

Heat together asparagus and mushroom soup, add cream and bring to just under a boil. Add lobster and heat through. Add sherry just before serving, heat a minute more, and sprinkle with chives.

Sea Food

Sea food is difficult to serve to company because, with a few notable exceptions (such as lobster, shrimp, or crabmeat), it requires considerable attention and does not improve by standing around waiting to be served. However, it is awfully good eating and many people (especially those who do not live by the sea) consider fish a delicacy. At our inn we have more requests for charcoal-broiled, fresh swordfish for birthday dinners than any other entrée. Except for swordfish, the quantities given for sea-food recipes are designed to serve four, in the hopes that you occasionally entertain friends who enjoy fish.

FILET OF SOLE

4 large (or 8 small) filets of sole
1 tablespoon minced onion
Dry white wine
16 cooked shrimp
16 mushrooms, sliced
2 tablespoons butter
Salt and fresh-ground pepper
2 teaspoons butter ⎫
⎬ kneaded together
2 teaspoons flour ⎭
Finely chopped chives (or parsley)
Lemon wedges

350-DEGREE OVEN

Arrange the sole in a shallow, buttered casserole (that has a lid). Sprinkle with onion and barely cover with wine. Scatter shrimp and mushrooms across the top, dot with butter, and season lightly with salt and pepper. Cover with buttered parchment (or wax) paper, then put on lid. Bake for 10 minutes in a 350-degree oven. Remove long enough to stir in kneaded butter and flour (blended together with fingers), put back in oven, covered, for another 10 minutes. Sprinkle with chives and serve with lemon wedges.

SAUTEED BAY SCALLOPS

1½ pounds bay scallops
1 egg
½ cup cold water
½ cup fine-herb bread
* crumbs*
Salt and fresh-ground
* pepper*

Paprika
4 tablespoons butter
* (more, if needed)*
½ cup dry white wine
Fresh, chopped parsley
4 slices bread, trimmed
4 lemon wedges

Wash scallops carefully and remove any adhering black particles. Drain well and dry on paper toweling. Beat egg and water together until well blended. Toss bread crumbs on

CRAB REMICK (for six)

2 cans crabmeat (7½
    ounces each)
6 slices crisp bacon
1 teaspoon dry mustard
½ teaspoon paprika

½ teaspoon celery salt
Few drops Tabasco sauce
1 teaspoon tarragon
    vinegar
1½ cups mayonnaise*

350-DEGREE OVEN

Flake crabmeat into a bowl and spoon into shallow, buttered, casserole. Place in 350-degree oven to warm (about 5 minutes). Meanwhile fry bacon until crisp, and blend together (in a bowl) mustard, paprika, celery salt, Tabasco, and vinegar. Lightly fold in mayonnaise and mix well. Remove casserole from the oven and arrange crisp bacon slices across the top, then spoon mayonnaise mixture over the entire dish. Brown under hot broiler (6 inches below) until bubbly and brown. Serve at once.

Poultry

BAKED HERB-BROILERS

2 tablespoons finely
    chopped chives
1 tablespoon finely
    chopped parsley
½ teaspoon finely
    chopped tarragon

If using dried
herbs, cut
quantity in half

¼ pound butter (at room temperature)
3 broilers (weighing about 1¾–2 pounds apiece)
¼ pound melted butter
Salt and fresh-ground pepper

500-DEGREE OVEN

Add herbs to the softened butter and blend well. Gently separate the skins of the broilers with fingers, just enough to be able to poke the herb butter under the skin and spread it over the under surface. Arrange broilers on an aluminum-foil-lined, closed cookie tin, skin side up, *not touching*. Melt butter, and brush on broilers; season with salt and pepper. Bake in 500-degree oven until crisply brown on the outside and tender inside (about 20–25 minutes). Baste occasionally.

CHICKEN BREASTS, AU GRATIN

*3 chicken breasts, split
    and boned*
½ cup flour
*Salt and fresh-ground
    pepper*

3 tablespoons butter
1 tablespoon oil
12 mushrooms, sliced thin
6 slices mozzarella cheese
Fresh, chopped parsley

Place boned chicken between sheets of wax paper and pound thin (with rolling pin, if nothing else is available). Place flour and seasonings in brown-paper bag and dredge chicken, shaking each piece well to eliminate excess flour. Heat butter and oil in heavy skillet, add chicken breasts, and sauté until tender (about 5–6 minutes on each side). Remove to buttered casserole. Sauté mushrooms in a little butter. Adjust seasoning of chicken, pour over sautéed mushrooms and cover each with a slice of cheese. Run under hot broiler until cheese is melted. Sprinkle lightly with parsley, and serve.

STUFFED TURKEY

There comes a time in every woman's life when the one perfect entrée for an occasion or a dinner party, is turkey, from which she instinctively shies. Turkeys are identified with Thanksgiving, big family reunions, groaning boards, and endless work. Although it's not that bad, you are indeed in the kitchen when preparing one. However, if tackle it you must (and you'll miss a lot if you don't)—here is the best recipe

I've ever found. While slaving away, keep in mind the sustaining thought of all the leftover dinners, salads, sandwiches, and soup that the future holds in store for you.

Giblets and neck
12–14-pound turkey
Salt and garlic salt
1 lemon, cut in two
Fresh-ground pepper

1 whole onion, sliced
¼ pound butter
1 cup dry white wine
1 cup giblet broth

350-DEGREE OVEN

HERB STUFFING

3 tablespoons butter
4 stalks celery, finely diced
1 small carrot, coarsely grated
3 tablespoons chopped, frozen onions
Salt and fresh-ground pepper

2 tablespoons chopped chives (or 1 tablespoon dried)
2 tablespoons chopped parsley (or 1 tablespoon dried)
2 cups coarse bread crumbs
1 cup chicken consommé
2 eggs

GRAVY

For added charm this gravy is not only superb, but can be made an hour or more before the turkey is done.

3 tablespoons butter
Ground giblets (grind in meat grinder)
1 tablespoon flour
Salt and fresh-ground pepper

Drippings from turkey (about 1¼ cups)
2 egg yolks
½ cup light cream
4 tablespoons Madeira

TO PREPARE STUFFING: Melt butter in a heavy skillet, add the vegetables, season with salt and pepper, and sauté for 15 minutes. Add herbs, crumbs, and consommé, mix well, and pour into a large bowl. Add eggs, lightly beaten.

TO PREPARE TURKEY: Cook giblets and neck in 2 cups of water until tender (for about 1 hour). Reserve the broth for basting the turkey (and thinning the gravy, if necessary), and grind the giblets (to be used in the gravy). Wash turkey thoroughly, inside and out. Sprinkle inside with salt and garlic salt (*no pepper*) from both ends. Take cut lemon and squeeze over entire *outside* surface, then sprinkle outside with salt, garlic salt, *and* pepper. Stuff loosely (stuffing expands during roasting) from both ends and sew up with trussing needle and twine (or use skewers). Add sliced onion to pan. Melt butter, add wine and 1 cup giblet broth, and pour over turkey. Put in 350-degree oven, uncovered, for 5½–6 hours. About every half hour baste and turn turkey from one side to the other—let stand breast side up for the last hour. If the drumsticks become very brown, baste them well and cover with aluminum foil. To test for doneness—grasp end of drumstick and if it moves easily, turkey is cooked through. Remove from oven, place on hot platter, and remove trussing. Cover with foil until ready to serve.

TO PREPARE THE GRAVY: Melt butter, add ground giblets, and brown. Add flour, salt and pepper to the pan, blend well, then 1¼ cups drippings from the roasting turkey. (There will be so much dripping in the pan that this can easily be spared.) Simmer 5 minutes. Meanwhile beat egg yolks in cream, add Madeira, blend well and add to gravy. Cook gently a few minutes more, then remove from fire until time to reheat and serve. (Adjust seasoning and add a little more dripping if you wish when reheating. Reputations have been made on this gravy alone.)

Meat

The recipes under this heading are planned for informal entertaining but, with the exception of Hamburger Diane, are still intended to keep you out front. Even Hamburger Diane can be assembled in the morning (through "shape mixture into 6 large patties") and cooked, come evening, in about ten minutes.

HAMBURGER DIANE

2 pounds chopped top round (or bottom, or chuck)
Salt and fresh-ground pepper
2 tablespoons chopped chives
2 tablespoons chopped parsley

1 teaspoon fresh lemon juice
Dash of Tabasco sauce
2 teaspoons Worcestershire sauce
3 tablespoons butter
4 tablespoons cognac
Chopped parsley for garnish

In a large bowl season meat with salt and pepper, then add chives, parsley, lemon juice, Tabasco, and Worcestershire sauce. Blend lightly and shape mixture into 6 large patties. Melt butter in a heavy skillet over high heat and brown first one side, then other. Reduce heat, and cook patties until medium rare (or whatever way preferred). Warm the cognac in a small saucepan, ignite, and, burning, pour over skillet. When fire dies down, transfer patties to a hot platter. Add a little fresh butter to the pan and stir briskly to dislodge all crisp particles. Pour hot sauce over patties, sprinkle with parsley, and serve.

LIZZIE'S POT ROAST   (Best made the day before!)

5-pound single brisket
Salt and fresh-ground pepper
Paprika
Ginger
Garlic powder
flour (¼–½ cup)
2 onions (sliced)
3–4 tablespoons fat
2 cups Burgundy wine

1 bay leaf
½ can tomato soup
Handful celery leaves
2 carrots
2 stalks celery
1 small onion
1 white turnip
1 teaspoon arrowroot
Fresh, chopped parsley

Rub the meat with a mixture of salt, pepper, paprika, ginger, garlic powder, and flour. Let stand, at room temperature, for 2 hours. Sauté sliced onions in fat in Dutch oven (or other heavy pan with lid). Add meat, and brown well on all sides. Add wine, bay leaf, tomato soup, celery leaves, and *1 carrot*, sliced. Cover pan and let simmer 4–5 hours (or ·until meat is tender). Remove meat from pan, strain gravy, and pour a little over the meat to keep it juicy. Pour remaining gravy into wide-mouthed jar, cool, and store in refrigerator to let fat solidify. Next day (or later the same day) remove fat before heating gravy. Finely chop the *other carrot*, celery, onion, and turnip. Cook vegetables in gravy until soft. Add arrowroot (mixed with 2 tablespoons cold stock or water) to thicken. Heat pot roast in a covered casserole on top of stove (or in 375-degree oven). Before serving, pour over a little hot gravy. *Do not strain gravy*—pour into gravy boat. Sprinkle pot roast with chopped parsley and serve.

KNACKWURST (OR FRANKFURTERS) AND SAUERKRAUT

12 knackwurst (or 12 frankfurters)
2 tablespoons bacon drippings (or butter)
2 large onions, sliced
1½ quarts sauerkraut
3 tart, medium-sized apples

1½ cups white wine
2 tablespoons vinegar
½ cup stock or bouillon
1 tablespoon dark-brown sugar
2 teaspoons celery seed

Drain sauerkraut. Heat bacon drippings in Dutch oven and sauté onions until transparent. Add the sauerkraut, stir well, and let cook slowly while peeling, coring, and dicing apples. Add apples, wine, vinegar, and stock to sauerkraut and cook slowly, uncovered, for 30 minutes. Add sugar and celery seed, mix well. Pierce knackwurst with a fork in several places and arrange on top of sauerkraut. Cover and bake in a 325-degree oven for 30–40 minutes.

MEAT LOAF MARY LYONS

2 pounds chuck, ground
2 tablespoons frozen,
    chopped onions
Salt and fresh-ground
    pepper
½ teaspoon dried orégano
1 teaspoon Worcestershire
    sauce
Shake of monosodium
    glutamate
Shake of seasoned salt

½ cup beef consommé
2 tablespoons fresh,
    chopped parsley
2 tablespoons fresh,
    chopped chives
2 raw eggs
¾ cup fine herb-
    bread crumbs
3 hard-cooked eggs
Catsup

350-DEGREE OVEN

In a large bowl and with a light hand, mix all the ingredients
except hard-cooked eggs and catsup. Shake catsup over bottom of loaf pan, copper pan, or any ovenproof dish. Firm
one half the meat in pan to form lower half of meat loaf and
spread the 3 eggs, lengthwise, on top. Cover with balance of
meat and bake in a 350-degree oven for 1 hour. Sprinkle with
parsley and serve. (When slicing, hard-cooked egg appears
in the middle of each slice.)

STUFFED HAM SLICES

4 tablespoons butter
1 large onion, finely
    chopped
12 mushrooms, finely
    chopped
1 teaspoon prepared
    mustard
¾ cup herb-bread crumbs

½–1 cup chicken stock
Salt and fresh-ground
    pepper
6 large slices of cold,
    boiled or baked ham,
    ¼ inch–½ inch thick
Chopped parsley

375-DEGREE OVEN

Heat one half of the butter in a skillet, add onion and mushrooms, and sauté until onions are soft but not browned. Add mustard, bread crumbs, and enough chicken stock to moisten the mixture and hold it together. Season to taste with salt and pepper, and spread mixture on ham slices. Fold slices in half and arrange on a shallow, buttered, baking dish. Melt balance of butter and brush lightly over top of ham slices. Cover with foil and bake in 375-degree oven for 20 minutes (or until piping hot). Remove foil, garnish with parsley and serve.

LAMB HAWAII

Boned leg of lamb (5–6 pounds)
Bones
Juice of 1 lemon
Salt and fresh-ground pepper
Ginger-garlic powder
¼ pound butter
1 carrot, finely diced

2 stalks celery, finely diced
2 tablespoons frozen, chopped onion
½ package herb stuffing
1 small can crushed pineapple
¼ cup capers

Two hours before roasting, remove lamb from refrigerator, wipe with paper toweling, and cut off excess fat. Brush inside and out with lemon juice, season with salt, pepper, and ginger-garlic, and let stand at room temperature. For the stuffing: melt butter in a saucepan and sauté vegetables for about 15 minutes. Add herb stuffing and pineapple, mix well, and spoon into lamb cavity. Tie up lamb around dressing with string and place on trivet in a roasting pan, with the bones on the bottom of the pan. Place in a 450-degree oven, uncovered, for 20 minutes. Reduce heat to 350 degrees and cover pan. Allow 30 minutes per pound, starting at this point. Baste occasionally. Make gravy with pan juices, unthickened, and just before serving add capers to the gravy. Adjust seasoning.

Salads

LOBSTER SALAD

This makes a fine hot-weather dinner, can be prepared in the morning, and assembled in 5 minutes just before dinner.

2 pounds cooked lobster meat

1 cup mayonnaise* (for this, homemade mayonnaise makes a great difference)

1 teaspoon curry powder (optional)

1 tablespoon grated onion

1 tablespoon chopped chives

2 tablespoons chopped parsley (reserve some for garnish)

4 hard-cooked eggs

½ cup diced celery (using white stalks only)

3 medium-sized, peeled, red tomatoes, cut into wedges

Salt and fresh-ground pepper

2 heads Bibb lettuce (or whatever you prefer)

Tart French dressing*

12 small lobster claws (for garnish, if you have cooked the lobsters yourself)

Cut lobsters into generous bite-sized pieces, and put in a large bowl. In a small bowl mix mayonnaise with curry powder, onion, chives, and 1 tablespoon parsley. Spoon 4 tablespoons of mayonnaise mixture over lobster, and turn gently to coat. Refrigerate lobster and balance of mayonnaise. In separate, small dishes, refrigerate hard-cooked eggs (chop two and slice two), diced celery, tomato wedges, and lobster claws. Wash and carefully dry salad greens, tear apart with fingers, and store in refrigerator in paper-towel-lined cellophane bag. Have French dressing ready, at room temperature. Just before serving, add chopped eggs, celery, and balance of mayonnaise to lobster and mix lightly. Toss salad greens in wooden bowl with French dressing (no excess—just enough to coat leaves). On a large platter make a bed of tossed lettuce and put tomatoes in the bowl vacated by the lettuce. Season them with salt and pepper and small residue of dressing. Mound lobster in center of platter on the lettuce, and place egg slices on the mound. Ring the salad with tomato wedges, arrange claws, and sprinkle everything with parsley.

JUNE'S GREEN SALAD

2 heads of lettuce,
  shredded with fingers
2 small cucumbers, sliced
  thin, unpeeled
½ red onion, sliced thin
Blue cheese (about the
  size of a marble)

Salt and fresh-ground
  pepper
2 tablespoons lemon juice
3 heaping tablespoons
  mayonnaise
Fresh, chopped parsley

Into a wooden salad bowl place lettuce, cucumbers, and onion. Over these crumble (or grate) the cheese. Season with salt and pepper and sprinkle lemon juice over the bowl. Add mayonnaise and toss lightly but thoroughly. Sprinkle with parsley.

TOMATO ASPIC WITH COTTAGE CHEESE

1 can (⅜2½) tomatoes
2 onions, sliced thin
1 bay leaf
1 teaspoon salt
6 whole cloves
6 peppercorns
2 tablespoons gelatin
½ cup cold water
2 tablespoons vinegar
1 tablespoon lemon juice

½ teaspoon sugar
1 pound cottage cheese
2 tablespoons chopped
  chives
3 tablespoons chopped
  parsley (reserve 1 for
  garnish)
1 tablespoon grated onion
Salt and fresh-ground
  pepper

Place first six ingredients in a pan and simmer for 30 minutes, then press through a strainer or food mill. Soften gelatin in cold water and dissolve in tomato mixture. Add vinegar, lemon juice, and sugar. Pour into lightly oiled ring mold, cool a little, then chill in refrigerator. In a bowl mix cottage cheese, chives, parsley, and onion. Season with salt and pepper. When aspic is partially set, add the cottage cheese, dropping it by tablespoon at equal distances apart. Continue to chill aspic until firm. Unmold on bed of salad greens that have been tossed in French dressing. Sprinkle parsley over platter. (Aspic can be made the day before using.)

SPRING SALAD

½ teaspoon dry mustard
½ teaspoon salt
Fresh-ground pepper
3 tablespoons vinegar
6 tablespoons salad oil
½ cup cooked string beans
½ cup cooked peas
4 sliced radishes

2 artichoke bottoms, cooked and sliced
2 hard-cooked eggs, coarsely chopped
1 teaspoon chopped chives
¼ cup mayonnaise*
2 teaspoons chopped parsley
4 cups young spinach, washed well and dried

In a wooden salad bowl, mix together mustard, salt, pepper, vinegar, and oil. Blend well. Add beans, peas, radishes, artichoke bottoms, eggs, and chives. Toss lightly together and marinate for at least an hour in refrigerator. Blend mayonnaise and 1 teaspoon parsley and add to vegetables. Arrange spinach leaves on a platter, salt lightly, and spoon over contents of the bowl. Sprinkle with balance of parsley.

CHICKEN SALAD

4 cups white meat of chicken, cut into bite-sized pieces
½ cup celery, coarsely chopped
1 cup seedless grapes
Salt and fresh-ground pepper
1 cup mayonnaise*
½–1 teaspoon curry powder (optional)

1 tablespoon grated onion
1 tablespoon chopped chives
2 tablespoons chopped parsley (reserve 1 for garnish)
2 concassed tomatoes*
2 small heads of lettuce
French dressing
¼ cup capers, drained

Combine the chicken, celery, grapes, salt and pepper. In a separate bowl blend together mayonnaise, curry powder, onion, chives, and parsley. Pour over chicken mixture and toss lightly. Put *concassed* tomatoes in wax paper on top of bowl and refrigerate until ready to serve. Break up lettuce with fingers in a wooden bowl and refrigerate. Have French dressing (see below) ready to use. When serving, toss lettuce and French dressing in wooden bowl, arrange on serving platter, and mound chicken salad in center. Toss *concassed* tomatoes in bowl and sprinkle around the sides. Scatter capers over the top and sprinkle with parsley.

FRENCH DRESSING

1 teaspoon salt	½ teaspoon sugar
½ teaspoon fresh-ground pepper	¼ cup lemon juice
½ teaspoon dry mustard	½ cup salad oil

Dissolve dry ingredients in lemon juice in a jar with screw-on top. Add oil. Shake well before using.

Vegetables

RED CABBAGE

Better if made the day before and reheated.

2 quarts water	4 tablespoons water
2 teaspoons salt	4 green apples (peeled, cored, and sliced)
1 medium-sized red cabbage	1 teaspoon sugar
2 tablespoons chopped, frozen onions	1 tablespoon butter
4 tablespoons vinegar	1 tablespoon flour

Bring water and salt to a boil. Remove outer leaves of cabbage; quarter and shred. Place in very large saucepan and pour the boiling salted water over it. Bring to a boil again. (The cabbage will turn purple, but the vinegar will bring back the red color.) Drain at once and pour into a well-buttered casserole. Add the chopped onion, a light sprinkling of salt, then the vinegar and water. Cover with buttered wax paper and the casserole lid and cook over medium heat (or in a 375-degree oven) for 30 minutes. Add apples and sugar, cover as before, and continue cooking for another 45 minutes. Add kneaded butter and flour to thicken. Mix well and cook for a minute or two more. Improves by being reheated the next day.

CAULIFLOWER TOSCANIA

1 large cauliflower
Boiling, salted water (to cover)
2 ounces butter
1 teaspoon chopped chives
6 medium-sized mushrooms, finely chopped

1 cup stock (chicken or beef)
2 egg yolks
2 ounces light cream
Salt and fresh-ground pepper
Fresh, chopped parsley

Break the cauliflower into flowerets (retaining a little green leaf) and drop into a pan of boiling salted water. Boil for 7 minutes, drain in colander. Heat ½ *of the butter* in the same pan, add chives, mushrooms, and stock. Blend well, and return cauliflower to pan. Cover with buttered wax paper and lid and simmer 15–20 minutes. Beat the egg yolks with the cream. Arrange cauliflower in a warm vegetable dish, and put in a warm place. Strain the stock in which cauliflower was cooked and add to egg yolks and cream. Heat over fire, careful not to let boil. Remove from fire, swirl in other half of butter, season to taste, add parsley to sauce, and spoon over cauliflower. Serve at once.

This same recipe is delicious substituting cucumbers for cauliflower. Wash and peel 3 cucumbers, cut down the middle and scoop out seeds. Cut into chunks. Continue as with cauliflower.

BAKED CORN CREOLE

(Can be prepared the day before or in the morning and baked at night.)

3 tablespoons butter	*2 cans young white,*
2 tablespoons frozen,	*whole-kernel corn,*
chopped onion	*drained*
½ green pepper	*Salt and fresh-ground*
(finely chopped)	*pepper*
1 tablespoon pimento	*Paprika*
(finely chopped)	*2 tablespoons light cream*
	350-DEGREE OVEN

Melt butter in skillet, add onion, green pepper, and pimento, and sauté over low heat for 5 minutes. Add corn, season to taste with salt and pepper, and sprinkle with paprika. Pour into buttered casserole or copper pan. Let stand until ready to bake (in refrigerator, if overnight). When ready to bake, spoon over the cream, cover with aluminum foil, and bake in 350-degree oven for 30 minutes.

SWEET AND SOUR BEANS

2 pounds green beans
4 quarts rapidly boiling water
6 teaspoons salt

SAUCE

1 tablespoon butter	*¼ cup sugar*
1 tablespoon flour	*¼ cup vinegar*
1 cup chicken or beef	*Salt and cayenne pepper*
consommé	*Fresh, chopped parsley*

Wash and trim beans and drop, slowly, into the boiling salted water. Bring water back to a boil over high heat, then reduce heat and boil slowly, uncovered, for about 12 minutes (or until slightly underdone). Drain beans and refresh* quickly under cold water. Turn into skillet and shake gently over moderate heat until remaining moisture has evaporated. Season with salt and pepper. Fold in the sauce, cover skillet, and simmer for 4–5 minutes. Spoon into hot vegetable dish, sprinkle with parsley, and serve.

TO PREPARE SAUCE: Heat butter in a saucepan, remove from stove and add flour. Return to stove and boil for a minute or two, then add consommé and stir until smooth and thickened. Add sugar, vinegar, and seasoning. Add to beans (see above).

Both beans and sauce can be prepared in the morning and assembled at dinnertime. When beans are cooked, run cold water over them for 2–3 minutes and spread on a clean towel to dry. When dry, put in a bowl in refrigerator. Cover and leave until ready to reheat—then drop beans into a large pan of rapidly boiling water, bring to a quick boil again, and drain at once. Shake in skillet as above and at the same time reheat sauce. Combine.

TOMATOES PROVENCALE

6 large red tomatoes
Salt and fresh-ground
    pepper
Pinch of sugar
4 tablespoons fine herb-
    bread crumbs

2 teaspoons finely
    chopped parsley
1 clove of garlic, minced
Olive oil

450-DEGREE OVEN

Cut tomatoes in half and gently shake out seeds and juice. Cut a sliver from the skin end of each so that it will stand straight. Season with salt, pepper, and tiny pinch of sugar on each half. In a small bowl mix together crumbs, parsley, and garlic. Dribble over a little oil—enough to hold mixture together, and spread on tomato halves. Arrange in a shallow, serving dish and bake in a 450-degree oven for 10 minutes (or place under broiler until crumbs are browned).

ZUCCHINI CASSEROLE

6 young, small, zucchini
1 tablespoon butter
1 tablespoon oil
1 clove of garlic, minced
2 tablespoons onion, finely
  chopped
1 tablespoon chopped
  chives
1 tablespoon celery, finely
  chopped
2 tablespoons chopped
  parsley (reserve 1 for
  garnish)

1 tablespoon chopped dill
  (or 1 teaspoon dried)
Salt and fresh-ground
  pepper
Paprika
1 cup canned, mixed
  vegetable juice
2 tablespoons catsup
½ teaspoon monsodium
  glutamate
½ teaspoon
  Worcestershire sauce
Parmesan cheese
375-DEGREE OVEN

Wash zucchini—*do not peel*—and cut into slices ½ inch thick. Melt butter and oil in heavy skillet and add garlic, onion, chives, celery, parsley, and dill. Season with salt, pepper, and paprika. Cook slowly until onions are soft. Combine vegetable juice, catsup, monosodium glutamate, Worcestershire sauce, and add to onion mixture. In a large casserole spread a little of the onion mixture and cover with slices of zucchini. Salt lightly, spoon over a little more onion mixture and sprinkle with Parmesan. Repeat layers, ending with sauce and cheese. Bake in 375-degree oven for one hour (or until tender).

ARTICHOKES POLONAISE

1 cup chicken stock
2 tablespoons butter
2 tablespoons finely
  chopped frozen onion

2 packages frozen
  artichoke hearts
  (partially defrosted)

SAUCE

2 ounces butter
¼ cup fine cracker
    crumbs
1 hard-cooked egg, finely
    chopped
4 tablespoons dry white
    wine

2 tablespoons catsup
¼ teaspoon onion powder
Salt and fresh-ground
    pepper to taste
1 tablespoon fresh,
    chopped parsley

TO PREPARE ARTICHOKES: Combine stock, butter, and onions in a saucepan and bring to a boil. Add artichokes, cover pan, and bring back quickly to a boil. Reduce heat and cook gently for 8–10 minutes (or until artichokes are tender). Uncover pan, raise heat to high and boil hard for 2 minutes. Drain well and spoon on to warm serving dish.

TO PREPARE SAUCE: While artichokes are cooking, heat butter in saucepan and add all other ingredients except parsley. Cook for 5 minutes over low heat and pour over artichokes on serving dish. Sprinkle with parsley.

Desserts

(A chocolate trio)

CHOCOLATE CUPS

Although the recipes in this chapter are designed for six, you can always dispose of a few "seconds"—hence nine. If you have never made them before, you will be scared. Again, trust me—they are truly a cinch.

9 ounces semisweet chocolate
3 tablespoons butter
9 paper baking cups (fluted)

FILLING

½ pint heavy cream
1 can (※2) chocolate
  syrup
Brandy to taste

Grated bitter chocolate
  (or chocolate
  sprinkle)

TO PREPARE CUPS: Melt chocolate in the top of double boiler over barely simmering water. Remove from stove when chocolate is melted. Add butter and stir with a wire whisk until well blended. Place paper cups in a muffin tin. Spoon chocolate into each cup—enough to cover bottom and crinkly sides (use back of spoon to press into crevices) until entire surface of cup is thinly coated. Place muffin tin in refrigerator to chill chocolate. It will harden again in about an hour.

TO PREPARE FILLING: Whip cream until very stiff, add chocolate syrup and brandy (to taste). Gently peel paper from chocolate cups (by pulling down a narrow strip from the top and then running it off sidewise). Arrange cups on platter and fill with syrup mixture. Sprinkle with grated chocolate and return to bottom shelf of refrigerator (protect by wax paper on shelf above) until ready to serve.

CHOCOLATE SPONGE   (Light, airy, and elegant)

1 tablespoon gelatin
¼ cup cold water
¾ cup boiling water
2 squares bitter chocolate
3 eggs, separated

½ cup sugar
Pinch of salt
1 teaspoon vanilla
½ pint whipping cream

Soak gelatin in cold water, add boiling water to dissolve. Melt chocolate in top of double boiler. Cool slightly. Beat egg yolks, sugar, and salt until thick and lemon-colored. Add gelatin, chocolate mixture, and vanilla. Blend well, then let stand in cool place (or bottom of refrigerator) until mixture begins to thicken (about 30 minutes), then beat egg whites until stiff and gently fold into mixture with a metal spoon. Pour into a lightly oiled ring mold and chill in refrigerator until firm (at least 4 hours—can be made the day before). Unmold on a serving platter (put platter, upside down over mold, and turn quickly, then place a hot rag on top and chocolate sponge will slide out). Whip cream, sweeten to taste, and either fill center or frost top and sides of ring. Sprinkle with grated chocolate—sweet or bitter.

(Whipped cream can be prepared hours ahead if kept in a bowl in the refrigerator, tightly covered with cellophane wrap or foil.)

FUDGE PIE

1 cup sugar
¼ pound butter (at room temperature)
2 eggs, separated
2 ounces bitter chocolate, melted

½ cup all-purpose flour (sifted before measuring)
1 teaspoon vanilla
Pinch of salt

325-DEGREE OVEN

TOPPING

1 pint vanilla (or coffee) ice cream
Chocolate sprinkle

Sift sugar. Place butter in mixing bowl and gradually add sugar, beating until mixture is well creamed. Beat in egg yolks and cooled, melted chocolate. Add flour and vanilla. Beat egg whites with pinch of salt until stiff, then lightly fold into batter with a metal spoon. Pour into an 8-inch greased pie plate and bake in 325-degree oven for 30–35 minutes. Just before serving, top with ice cream and chocolate sprinkle.

SPONGECAKE

This one is really Dessert Unlimited, for with a wave of the hand it can be turned into peach shortcake, strawberry short-cake, chocolate cake, mocha cake, etc., etc. It is easy to make and lovely to have on hand in the freezer.

6 ounces all-purpose flour   *1 cup sugar*
Pinch of salt   *⅛ teaspoon cinnamon*
4 eggs

375-DEGREE OVEN

Sift flour 3 times with salt. Break eggs into a bowl (much easier if you have a mixer for this one), add sugar and beat together until thick and mousselike (about 10 minutes in the electric mixer while you do something else). It is done when, tested with a spoonful dropped back, it makes a thick ribbon on itself. Using a metal spoon, cut and fold flour into mixture, lightly, but make sure all is blended. Turn into two 8-inch paper-lined prepared cake tins and bake 25–30 minutes in 375-degree oven. When done (test with a cake tester—or broom straw as last resort), run a knife around edges, cover with wire cakeracks, and turn upside down. Quickly peel off paper lining. When cool, turn cake bottomside down.

TO MAKE STRAWBERRY SHORTCAKE

1 quart strawberries
Sugar to taste
½ pint whipping cream, whipped

Reserve a dozen of the best berries for garnish and slightly crush the balance. Sweeten to taste and let stand at room temperature (or warm slightly in low oven) before adding to cake. Spread half the fruit over one layer, top with the other. Mix second half of crushed berries with *one-half* of the whipped cream and spread over top. Frost sides with the balance of the whipped cream. Decorate top with reserved berries.

TO MAKE PEACH SHORTCAKE

1 can (⚹2½) old-fashioned, sliced peaches
  or 5 cups sliced fresh peaches.
  With the canned it is a year-round dessert
  and very good.

APRICOT GLAZE

>*6 tablespoons apricot preserves*
>*1 tablespoon fresh lemon juice*
>*½ pint whipping cream, whipped*

Drain peaches thoroughly.

TO PREPARE THE GLAZE: Melt apricot jam over medium heat. When boiling, strain into another pan and return to stove for 2 minutes, again over medium heat. Add lemon juice and blend.

TO ASSEMBLE CAKE: Place one layer on serving platter, brush lightly with glaze. Combine one half whipped cream with about one third of the peaches, and spread over this layer. Cover with other layer and lightly brush with glaze. Arrange remaining peaches, overlapping, to within 1 inch of outer edge. Pile slightly higher in the middle. Brush peaches lavishly with remainder of glaze, and pipe remaining whipped cream around outer edge (or swirl with spoon).

CARAMEL ICING

>*4 cups dark-brown sugar*
>*1 cup milk*
>*¼ pound butter*
>
>*1 teaspoon vanilla*
>*Grated bitter chocolate*

Place sugar, milk, and butter in a saucepan and cook over medium heat until it forms a firm ball when dropped in cold water. Remove from heat and beat about 4 minutes (or until on scraping the sides, it does not run and is right consistency for spreading). Ice one layer, cover with the other and repeat. Sprinkle grated bitter chocolate across the top.

LEMON ICING

>*2 unbeaten egg whites*
>*1½ cups sugar*
>*3 tablespoons cold water*
>*1½ teaspoons light corn syrup*
>
>*¼ teaspoon cream of tartar*
>*2 tablespoons lemon juice*
>*1 teaspoon grated lemon rind*

In the top of a double boiler place the egg whites, sugar, water, corn syrup, and cream of tartar. Beat until well blended. Place over rapidly boiling water and beat with rotary electric beater (or hand beater) for 7 minutes. Remove from fire and continue beating until frosting is thick enough to spread (another 2–3 minutes*). Add lemon juice, and ice cake (swirling top layer to give interest). Garnish with grated lemon rind.

(The variations are endless—raspberries, treated like strawberries, chocolate, orange, or mocha frosting etc., etc.)

LEMON CHARLOTTE

This dessert looks especially handsome if made in a medium-sized springform, although it tastes just as wonderful spooned out of a soufflé dish or anything else you happen to have. Don't let it scare you.

2 packages ladyfingers
1 ounce gelatin
4 tablespoons fresh lemon juice
5 eggs

½ cup sugar
Pinch of salt
2 teaspoons grated lemon peel
½ pint whipping cream

SAUCE

3 tablespoons apricot preserves
3 tablespoons orange marmalade
Juice of 1 orange

1 tablespoon fresh lemon juice
2 tablespoons butter
¼ cup slivered, toasted almonds

Separate the ladyfingers and cover bottom and sides of springform, cutting them to fit tightly over the bottom and arranging them to stand up around the sides (can be as much as 1 inch above rim). Take a long piece of aluminum foil (long enough to go generously around the springform) and fold three times the long way. Tie around dish—this will protect ladyfingers when you pour in the filling.

Dissolve the gelatin in lemon juice and melt over hot water.

Place the eggs, sugar, and salt in the top of double boiler over *simmering* water. Beat (with portable electric beater or hand one) until the mixture is thick and very light in color (4–5 minutes). Add the melted gelatin and lemon peel, beat a few seconds more. Cool for a few minutes, then whip the cream and fold in with care (volume will diminish a little). Pour entire contents into prepared springform. *Refrigerate overnight.* (This can be made first thing in the morning on the day of a dinner party, but how much easier the day before.)

TO PREPARE SAUCE: Melt together over a low fire apricot preserves, orange marmalade, orange and lemon juice. In a separate small pan melt butter, add almonds, and sauté until lightly browned. Add almonds to sauce, blend well, and place in sauceboat. Can be served warm or at room temperature. Just before guests arrive, remove Charlotte from refrigerator and carefully remove rim. Put on serving platter. The ladyfingers stand above the cake, looking attractive and making slicing easy.

KUCHEN

Quick and delicious—fine for emergencies and just as good when there are none.

2 cups biscuit mix	1 cup dark-brown sugar
⅔ cup light cream	1 cup chopped nuts
10 ounces melted butter	(pecans or walnuts)
1 tablespoon sugar	1 tablespoon cinnamon

400-DEGREE OVEN

In a large bowl combine lightly together biscuit mix, cream, *2 ounces melted butter*, and white sugar. Grease a closed cookie tin, divide batter into 6 or 8 parts and place on tin. Lightly flour palms of hands and pat batter until entire cookie tin is covered with thin pastry. Sprinkle brown sugar and nuts over entire surface, sprinkle over with cinnamon, and then spoon over the remaining 8 ounces melted butter (moving fast up and down so that a little butter goes over the whole pan). Bake in a 400-degree oven for 15 minutes. Cut into large squares while still hot, but let remain in pan until cool.

Ice Cream

As previously suggested, filling an oiled mold with a mixture of ice cream can produce a quick, delicious dessert. Serving *crème de cacao*, cointreau, or Grand Marnier with vanilla; brandy with chocolate; green crème de menthe with pineapple (or lemon) sherbet; or a dash of orange Curaçao with orange ice adds interest and flavor. But if you happen to like sweet sauces, try these:

CHOCOLATE SAUCE

1 cup granulated sugar
½ cup milk
2 squares bitter chocolate

1–2 tablespoons sherry
(optional)

Place sugar, milk, and chocolate in a pan, bring to a boil, and boil 3½ minutes. Remove from stove, beat for 1 minute and add sherry. Serve hot, warm, or cold.

BUTTERSCOTCH SAUCE

1 cup light-brown sugar
½ cup light corn syrup
3 tablespoons butter
Dash of salt

½ teaspoon vanilla
½ cup light cream (or
*   evaporated milk)*

Simmer sugar, corn syrup, butter, and salt over moderate heat until mixture forms a firm ball in cold water. Remove from stove, add vanilla and cream. Serve hot, warm, or cold.

Fruit Desserts

PINEAPPLE STUFFED WITH STRAWBERRIES

1 *large pineapple*   *Instant superfine sugar*
1 *quart fresh strawberries*   *kirsch to taste*

Cut pineapple in half, lengthwise. Remove the core and cut out the fruit. Slice into bite-sized pieces. Wash and hull strawberries and combine the two fruits in a crockery bowl. Add sugar to taste, then kirsch (start with 2 tablespoons). Marinate the fruit in the refrigerator for a few hours. Serve fruit in the pineapple shell or in a glass bowl. Have at room temperature an hour before serving. Sprinkle with powdered sugar just before serving.

CHERRIES ESCOFFIER

½ *pound pitted tart*   *Grated rind and juice of 1*
   cherries   *orange*
2 *tablespoons sugar*   3 *tablespoons red-currant*
Pinch of cinnamon   *jelly*
1 *cup Burgundy*

Place pitted cherries in a saucepan, add sugar and cinnamon, and cook over low heat until juices start to run (about 5 minutes). In a separate pan cook the Burgundy until it is reduced by one half, add the orange rind and juice and jelly, and stir until jelly has melted. Add the cherries and simmer for 3–4 minutes. Cool, then chill in refrigerator until ready to serve.

(This is very good served with a bowl of sour cream, with a pinch of cinnamon across the top.)

PEACHES CARMEN

For this dessert only fresh peaches will do.

1 quart fresh raspberries   *1 tablespoon kirsch*
2–3 ounces confectioners'   *6 large ripe peaches*
  sugar

Gently wash and thoroughly drain raspberries. Sieve them into a bowl, then gradually work the sugar and kirsch into the purée. Set aside. Peel the peaches and place at once in a glass bowl. Spoon over the raspberry purée and chill in refrigerator until about half an hour before serving.

STRAWBERRIES IN ORANGE CREAM

2 bright-colored oranges   *½ pint whipping cream*
Stainless steel grater   *1–2 tablespoons brandy*
2 tablespoons orange juice   *1 quart fresh strawberries,*
2 tablespoons   *washed and hulled*
  confectioners' sugar

Grate oranges (on finest blade of grater) into a bowl. Add orange juice and sugar and blend well. To the whipped cream (in a separate bowl) add the orange mixture and brandy. In a glass fruit bowl layer first strawberries, then orange cream, ending with the cream. Chill in refrigerator until just before serving.

FIGS AND SOUR CREAM (Quick and good.)

2 large cans Kadota figs   *1 cup sour cream*
Crème de cacao to taste   *Sugar*
  (start with 2   *Cinnamon*
  tablespoons)

Drain figs well and chill. Add a little crème de cacao to sour cream, sweeten with a little sugar. Place chilled figs in glass serving bowl and cover top with sour-cream combination so that figs are concealed. Sprinkle cinnamon over top and refrigerate until ready to serve.

PEACHES GLAMOUR   (Also quick and very good.)

*6 canned cling peach
 halves
¼ cup brown sugar
1 tablespoon butter
¼ cup ground ginger
 snaps*

*½ teaspoon grated lemon
 rind
1 tablespoon syrup from
 peaches
Sour cream
Cinnamon*

350-DEGREE OVEN

Drain peaches and place, cup side up, in a shallow baking dish.
Combine sugar, butter, ginger snaps, lemon rind, and syrup
in a small bowl, and press with a fork until thoroughly blended.
Fill peaches with mixture. Bake in a 350-degree oven for 25
minutes. When cooled, place a small dollop of sour cream in
the center of each and sprinkle with cinnamon. (Or serve
sour cream separately.)

Cookies

CHOCOLATE MERINGUE COOKIES

We have yet to serve these without being asked for the
recipe. They are glossy, chewy, and delicious.

*2 egg whites
½ cup sugar
6-ounce package chocolate
 bits, melted and
 cooled*

*½ teaspoon vanilla
¾ cup chopped nuts*

350-DEGREE OVEN

Beat egg whites until almost stiff, then slowly add sugar. Beat
mixture until stiff and smooth. Add melted, cooled chocolate,
vanilla, and nuts. Drop by spoonfuls, 2 inches apart, on a
greased, and lightly floured cookie tin. Bake 12 minutes in
350-degree oven. Cool for 2 minutes, then remove to platter.
Makes about 18.

MERINGUE SUGAR COOKIES

These are more like cake squares and very good.

½ cup butter

1 cup sugar

1 egg (well beaten)

1 tablespoon cream

½ teaspoon vanilla

1½ cups all-purpose flour

¼ teaspoon salt

1 teaspoon baking powder

MERINGUE

1 egg white

1 cup brown sugar

½ teaspoon vanilla

½ cup chopped pecans or
walnuts (optional)

Cream butter, add sugar, egg, cream, and vanilla. Sift together flour, salt, and baking powder, and fold into mixture. When well blended, spread mixture evenly in a buttered, shallow 9 inch by 9 inch pan.

TO PREPARE THE MERINGUE: Beat egg white until quite stiff, add brown sugar and vanilla. Continue beating for 1 minute more, then spread over the cookie mixture, covering the entire surface. Sprinkle with chopped nuts and bake in a 325-degree oven for 35 minutes. Cut in squares while still warm.

BEST DATE BARS

These provide an answer to what to do with those egg yolks left over after making meringue desserts.

1 cup sugar

¼ pound butter

½ teaspoon vanilla

Pinch salt

5 or 6 egg yolks

2 tablespoons ice water

1½ cups cake flour

¼ teaspoon ground cloves

½ teaspoon ground
cinnamon

2 cups chopped dates

½ cup chopped nuts

Powdered sugar

325-DEGREE OVEN

Sift sugar. Cream butter until soft, then slowly add sugar, beating until creamy and well blended. Add vanilla and salt. In a separate bowl beat egg yolks until blended, then add water. Stir yolks into butter mixture. Sift together flour, cloves, and cinnamon. Stir gradually into batter. Add dates and nuts. Spread mixture in a buttered and lightly floured 9 inch by 13 inch pan. Bake in a 325-degree oven for 30–35 minutes (or until a light brown). Let cool, then cut into bars. Sprinkle with powdered sugar before serving.

MARIE'S COOKIES

Requires 5 minutes to make. Irresistible, alas.

1 egg, beaten	2 ounces butter
1 cup dark-brown sugar	½ teaspoon vanilla
Pinch of salt	½ cup chopped nuts
¼ cup all-purpose flour	1½ cups puffed rice

325-DEGREE OVEN

Combine the first six ingredients and blend well. In a separate bowl mix nuts and puffed rice, add to mixture and stir together. Drop by teaspoonfuls on a greased and lightly floured cookie tin, 2 inches apart. Press down with the back of a fork. Bake in a 325-degree oven for 10 minutes (or until brown). Remove from oven and, at once, loosen one end of each cookie with a spatula. Then let set for 2–3 minutes. Starting at loosened end, they will come off the cookie tin easily. Makes about 30.

ADDIE'S CHOCOLATE BROWNIES

2 squares bitter chocolate	½ cup all-purpose flour,
2 ounces butter	unsifted
1 cup sugar	½ cup chopped nuts
2 eggs	1 teaspoon vanilla
Pinch of salt	

300-DEGREE OVEN

Melt chocolate in top of double boiler over hot water. Remove from fire, add butter and stir with wire whisk until melted. Add sugar, eggs, salt, and flour, and mix well. Add nuts and vanilla. Grease and flour an 8 inch by 8 inch pan and spread batter evenly. Bake in a 300-degree oven for 40–45 minutes. Cool and cut into squares.

CRESCENTS

¼ *pound sweet butter*
2 *tablespoons powdered sugar*
1 *cup all-purpose flour, sifted*
Pinch of salt

1 *teaspoon water*
1 *cup pecans, finely chopped*
1 *teaspoon vanilla*
Powdered sugar for garnish

350-DEGREE OVEN

Cream butter, add sugar and blend well. Sift together flour and salt and add to mixture. Add water, nuts, and vanilla, and mix well. Take by teaspoonfuls and shape into curved crescents. Place on lightly greased cookie tin and bake in a 350-degree oven for about 30 minutes or until a pale brown. Before serving, sprinkle with powdered sugar. Makes about 18.

SPICE REFRIGERATOR COOKIES

These freeze very well and defrost enough to slice for baking in 20 minutes.

¼ *pound butter*
¼ *pound margarine*
½ *cup brown sugar*
½ *cup granulated sugar*
1 *egg*
2¼ *cups sifted all-purpose flour*
½ *teaspoon soda*

½ *teaspoon salt*
2 *teaspoons cinnamon*
¼ *teaspoon cloves*
¼ *teaspoon nutmeg*
½ *cup finely chopped nuts*
Powdered sugar for sprinkling

375-DEGREE OVEN

Cream together shortening and sugars; add egg and beat well. Sift together dry ingredients and stir into creamed mixture. Add nuts. Shape into rolls about 2½ inches in diameter. Chill dough for an hour in refrigerator before baking. When ready to bake, slice very thin (about ⅛ inch). Bake 1 inch apart on lightly greased cookie tin in 375-degree oven for 5–7 minutes (or until a medium brown). Remove at once from pan. Makes about 60. When ready to serve, sprinkle with powdered sugar.

PATSY'S COOKIES

This amount will make an enormous number of cookies. Suggest that you freeze balance of dough after baking as much as you want.

1 pound butter (at room
    temperature)
1 cup light-brown sugar

2 egg yolks (beaten
    together)
1 teaspoon vanilla
4 cups cake flour, sifted
300-DEGREE OVEN

Cream butter and add sugar. Beat until well blended. Add egg yolks and mix well. Add vanilla and, finally, flour. Pat into a ball and refrigerate for at least an hour. When ready to bake, roll out part of the dough (on a lightly floured board) very thin, and cut out circles with a 2-inch cutter. Then, using a 1-inch cutter, cut one half the circles in the center, putting the cut-out dough back in the ball. Cover center of larger circles with various jams (strawberry, apricot, orange marmalade, etc.), then cover with a round with a hole in the center. (If a little jam goes under between the two, it will help keep the rounds together.) Press them lightly together and bake in a 300-degree oven for 15 minutes.

PECAN COOKIES

2 tablespoons flour
2 cups dark-brown sugar
2 egg whites

1½ teaspoons vanilla
1½ cups chopped pecans

325-DEGREE OVEN

Work flour into sugar with fingers (in a large bowl). Add the stiffly beaten egg whites. Fold in vanilla and pecans. Drop by teaspoonfuls on a greased and lightly floured cookie sheet. Bake 15 minutes in a 325-degree oven. Loosen one end of each cookie, then let cool for about 3 minutes. Remove from pan with spatula. Makes about 24.

Miscellaneous Recipes

AUNT FAN'S EGGS   (For 4)

4 slices imported Swiss cheese

Prepared mustard (your choice)

8 eggs (at room temperature)

Salt and fresh-ground pepper

Parmesan cheese

2 tablespoons heavy cream

Lightly butter 4 shallow, individual baking dishes (or 1 large baking dish) and line with Swiss cheese. Spread with mustard, and gently break eggs (two to a person) and slide on to cheese. Season with salt and pepper, sprinkle with Parmesan cheese, and dribble over ½ tablespoon cream per portion. Bake in a 325-degree oven for about 20 minutes (or until eggs are set).

BANANA BREAD

⅓ cup vegetable shortening

⅔ cup sugar

2 eggs

1¾ cups all-purpose flour

2 teaspoons baking powder

¼ teaspoon soda

3 overripe bananas

½ cup chopped walnuts

350-DEGREE OVEN

Cream together vegetable shortening and sugar. Add eggs, one at a time, and blend well. Sift together flour, baking powder, and soda. Add to mixture and blend well. Mash bananas (in the blender if you have one) and add them and nuts to mixture. Pour into a buttered, floured, bread pan. Bake in a 350-degree oven for 50 minutes.

CHEESE SOUFFLE (For 4)

4 tablespoons butter	Dash of cayenne pepper
4 tablespoons flour	½ teaspoon
1 cup milk	Worcestershire sauce
2 cups grated, sharp	½ teaspoon dry mustard
Cheddar cheese	4 egg yolks
Salt and fresh-ground	5 egg whites
pepper	

In a saucepan melt butter over medium heat, remove from fire, and blend in flour. Bring milk to just under a boil. Return pan to fire, add hot milk all at once, stirring vigorously with a wire whisk until sauce is thickened and smooth. Remove from heat and add grated cheese, stirring until melted. Season to taste with salt, pepper, cayenne, and then add balance of seasonings. Cool slightly. Beat egg yolks until well blended and add to mixture. Mix well.

(This much can be done hours ahead but the mixture must not be left in an aluminum pan as the eggs will turn black. Pour into a crockery bowl, cover with wax paper just touching mixture—to avoid scum—and let stand.)

When ready to bake—beat egg whites until stiff, lightly fold into cheese mixture and pour into 2-quart soufflé dish. Bake in 425-degree oven for 30 minutes. (No harm if it must stay in an extra ten or fifteen minutes if you do *not* open the oven door. Once removed from oven, serve at once.)

YELLOW PLUM-TOMATO PRESERVE

2 quarts yellow plum tomatoes	3 teaspoons ground ginger
	8 cups sugar
1 lemon, (cut into paper-thin slices, then cut in half)	1 cup water
	8 sterilized pint jars

Wash tomatoes (do *not* peel). Lightly oil a large pan (this will prevent the fruit from sticking to the bottom) and combine all the ingredients in the pan. Cook until tomatoes have a clear look and the syrup is about as thick as honey (about 35–40 minutes). Cool, fill jars, seal, and store.

HERB TOAST

Especially good with lobster, fish, or chicken.

10 slices close-grained white bread
¼ pound butter
2 cloves of garlic, squeezed through press
1 teaspoon fresh lemon juice
½ teaspoon crumbled, dried orégano
½ teaspoon Worcestershire sauce
Salt and fresh-ground pepper
1 teaspoon chopped parsley

Trim the crusts off the bread. Melt butter in a small pan and add all ingredients. Arrange bread on closed cookie tin, brush with butter mixture, and toast under broiler. Turn, brush other side with butter mixture and, just before serving, toast second side under broiler.

ICED TEA

We make it by the gallon and never have enough on hand.

20 cups of water
10 oranges
7 lemons
1 cup orange pekoe tea
1 large bunch fresh mint
3 cups sugar

Bring water to a boil. Meanwhile squeeze oranges and lemons, deposit rinds of both in large pan, and strain juice of both into one pitcher. Add tea and mint to rinds, and when water is boiling, pour into this pan of tea, rinds, and mint. Let stand 1 hour. Remove rinds by squeezing them with hands and shaking juice into pan. Strain contents of pan into another large pan, add sugar and strained fruit juice and stir until sugar is melted. Let cool, bottle, and refrigerate. When serving, shake well and pour contents *over ice in glasses*. If ice is added to pitcher, this delicious drink is diluted.

STUFFED SANDWICH ROLLS

2 cups cooked chicken, diced
4 hard-cooked eggs, coarsely chopped
¼ cup sweet-pickle relish
2 teaspoons prepared mustard (your choice)
½ cup mayonnaise
½ teaspoon curry powder (optional)
Salt and fresh-ground pepper
12 frankfurter rolls
Butter

Combine all the ingredients in a bowl and blend well. Season to taste with salt and pepper. Slice off top of each roll, scoop out soft bread, and spread inside shell with butter. Fill rolls with well-seasoned mixture and replace tops. Wrap individually in aluminum foil and refrigerate. *To serve hot*—place wrapped, in a 350-degree oven for 25 minutes. Can be served cold, and are especially nice to take on picnics (right in the foil).

Your recipe box is more than a file. It is a memory book that brings back friendships and adventure, sadness and gladness, good cheer and gaiety. For food, basic and indispensable though it may be, gives fusion and harmony to our lives. It brings us together in warmth and hospitality, thaws loneliness, unites families, accelerates friendship. It reaches out to the senses with fragrance, color, texture, and taste. It offers comfort and satisfaction.

And so—good appetite and happy cooking!

INDEX

Index